RECORDED VERSIONS GUITAR

AUTHENTIC TRANSCRIPTIONS
WITH NOTES AND TABLATURE

W9-CHK-354

CONTENTS

Music transcriptions by Pete Billmann, Colin Higgins,
Jeff Jacobson and Jeff Story

ISBN 0-634-05790-1

HAL•LEONARD®
CORPORATION

7777 W. BLUEMOUND RD. P.O. BOX 13819 MILWAUKEE, WI 53213

In Australia Contact:
Hal Leonard Australia Pty. Ltd.
22 Taunton Drive P.O. Box 5130
Cheltenham East, 3192 Victoria, Australia
Email: ausadmin@halleonard.com

Visit Hal Leonard Online at
www.halleonard.com

The Hell Song

Words and Music by Sum 41 and Greig Andrew Nori

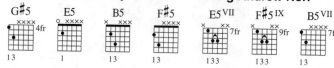

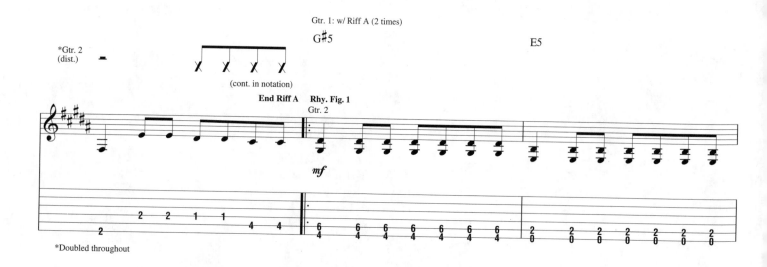

*Doubled throughout

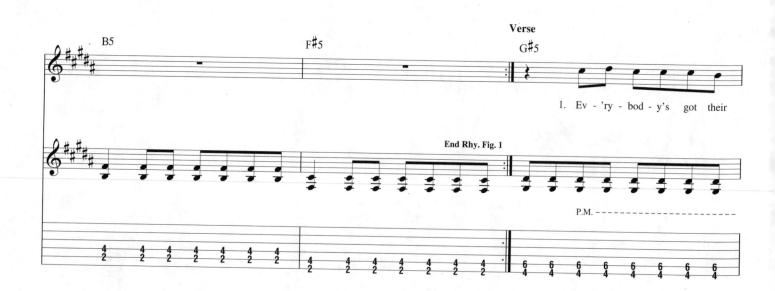

1. Ev - 'ry - bod - y's got their

see what's go - ing on. I can't be - lieve this hap-pened to

End Rhy. Fig. 4

P.M. --⌐   P.M. ------⌐   P.M. f

Interlude

Gtr. 1: w/ Riff A (2 times)
Gtr. 2: w/ Rhy. Fig. 1 (2 times)

you. ____

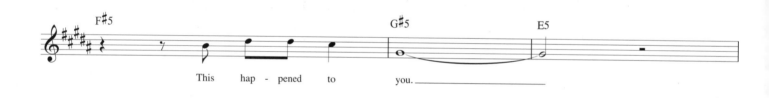

This hap - pened to you. ____

Verse

2. It's just a prob - lem that we're

Gtr. 1

Gtr. 2

P.M. ----⌐   P.M. ---------⌐   P.M. ----

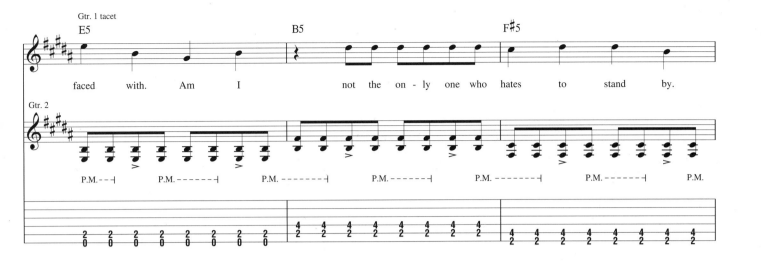

faced with. Am I not the on-ly one who hates to stand by.

Com - pli - ca - tions end - ed first in this line. With all these pic - tures run - ning

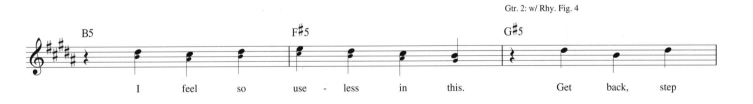

through my mind. Know - ing end - less con - se - quenc - es.

I feel so use - less in this. Get back, step

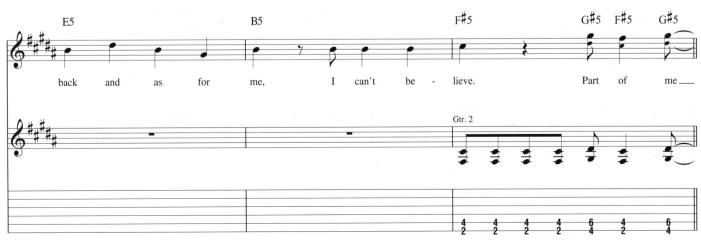

back and as for me, I can't be - lieve. Part of me ___

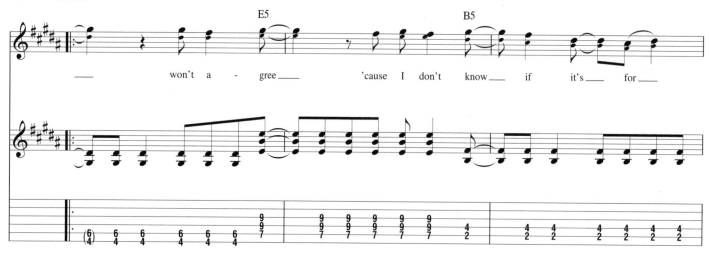

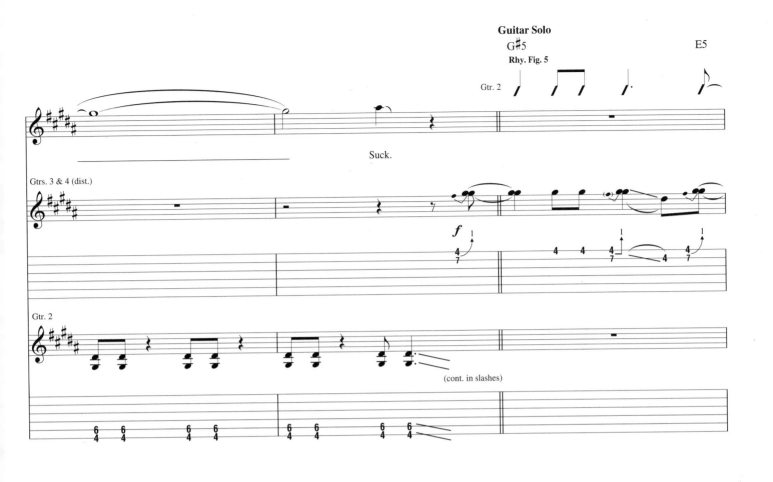

Guitar Solo

Suck.

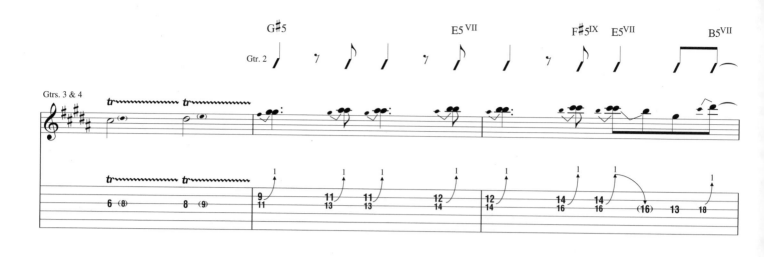

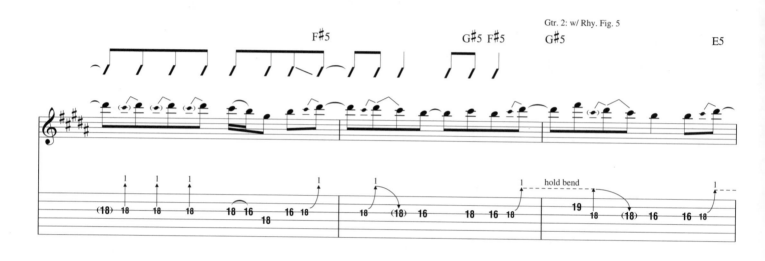

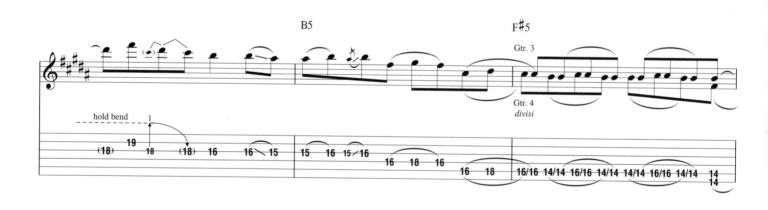

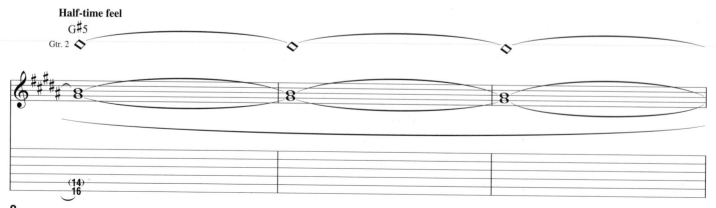

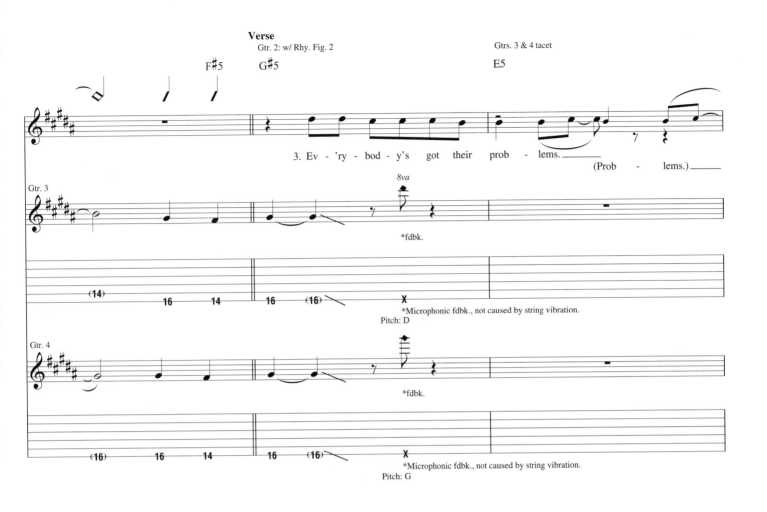

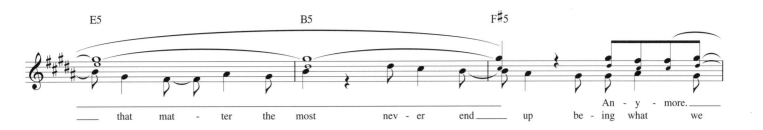

that mat - ter the most nev - er end_____ up be - ing what we

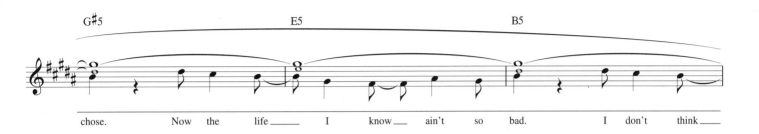

chose.   Now the life _____ I know ___ ain't so bad.   I don't think ___

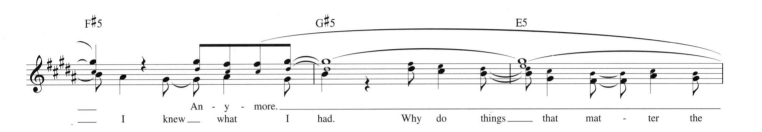

An - y - more. _____

___ I knew ___ what I had.   Why do things ___ that mat - ter the

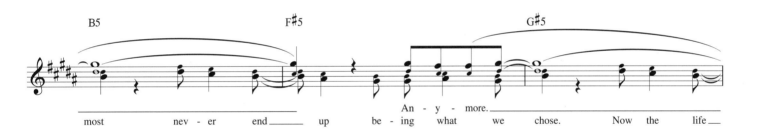

An - y - more. _____

most   nev - er end _____ up be - ing what we chose.   Now the life ___

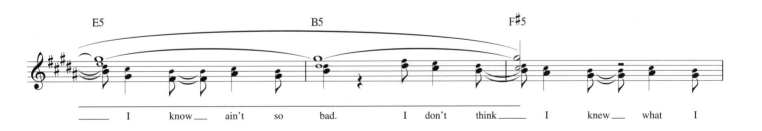

___ I know ___ ain't so bad.   I don't think ___ I knew ___ what I

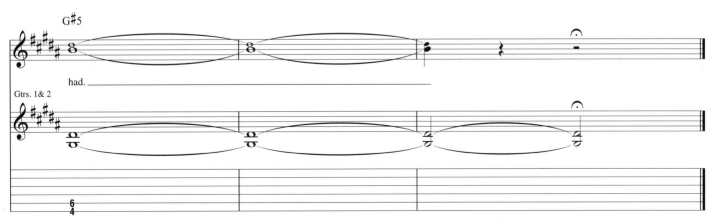

had. _____

Gtrs. 1 & 2

Over My Head (Better Off Dead)

Words and Music by Sum 41 and Greig Andrew Nori

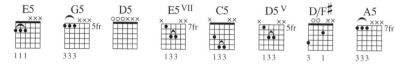

Drop D tuning:
(low to high) D-A-D-G-B-E

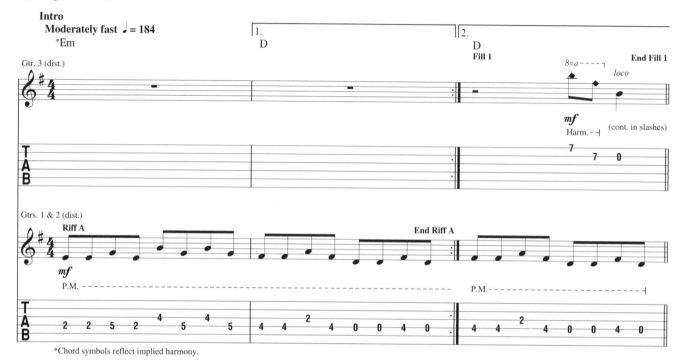

*Chord symbols reflect implied harmony.

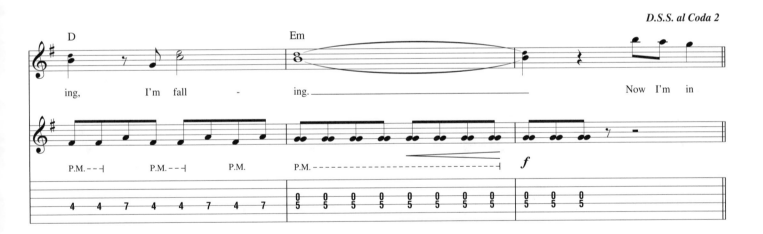

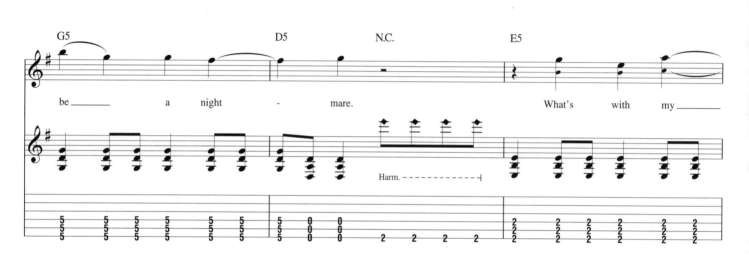

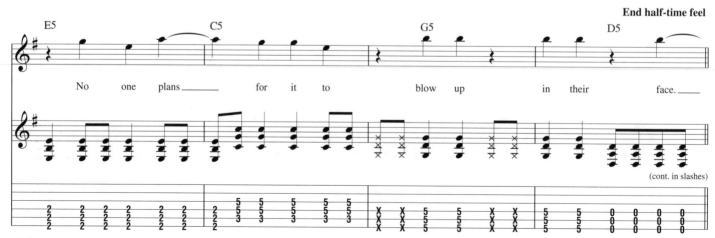

Interlude

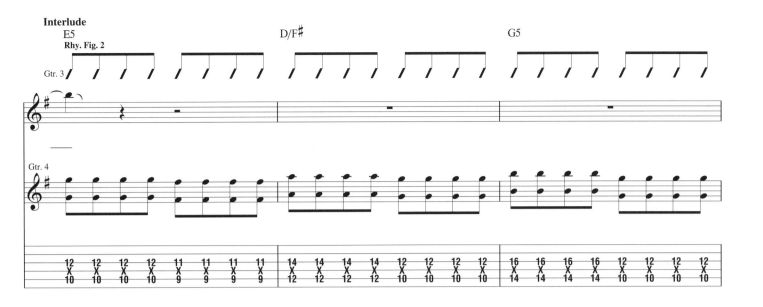

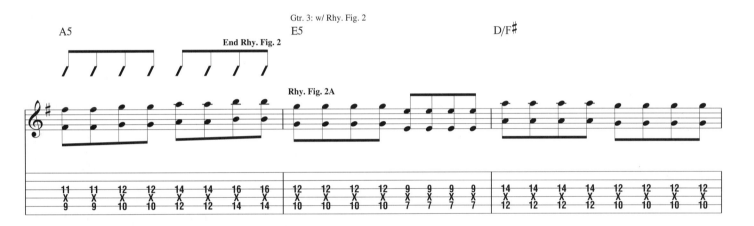

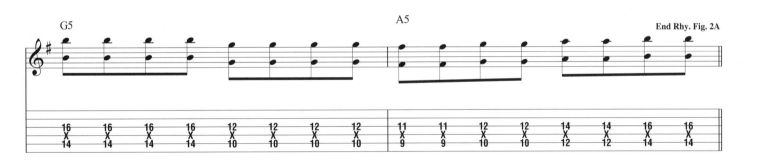

Pre-Chorus

Gtrs. 3 & 4: w/ Rhy. Figs. 2 & 2A (2 times)

Who said it was eas - y

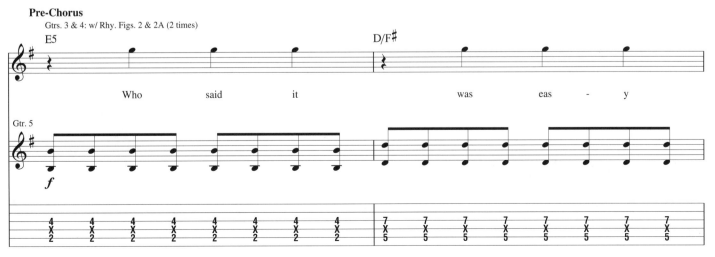

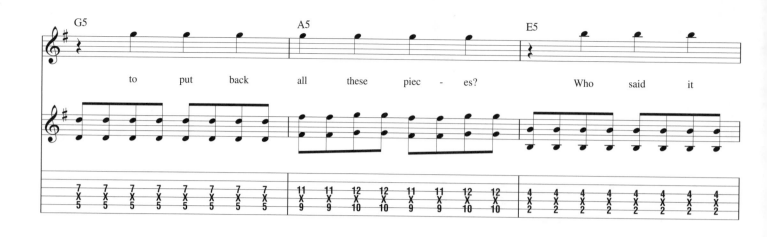

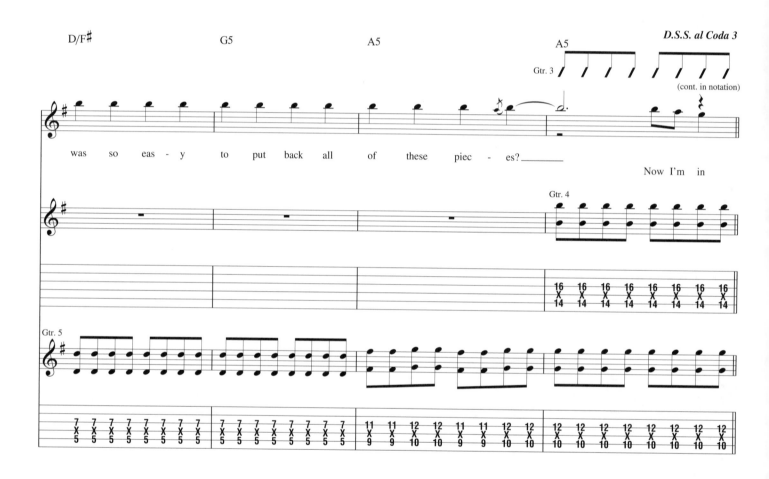

Coda 3

Outro

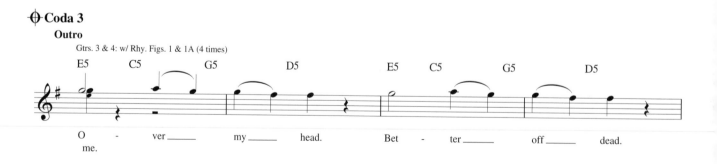

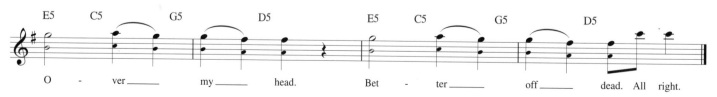

My Direction

Words and Music by Sum 41 and Greig Andrew Nori

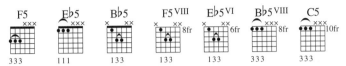

Drop D tuning:
(low to high) D-A-D-G-B-E

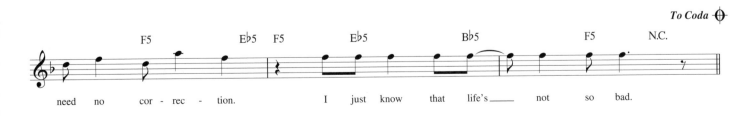

Verse
Double-time feel

1. Pic - ture this, ev - 'ry - day, kids that just can't find a way. Stuck in dis - ar - ray, can't find

hope for bet - ter days. It's the de - gen - er - a - tion of child - hood frus - tra - tion.
Spoken: In the

D.S. al Coda
End double-time feel

last thirty years teenage suicide has increased three hundred percent in North America; it is the second major cause of death in Canada.

Coda
Interlude

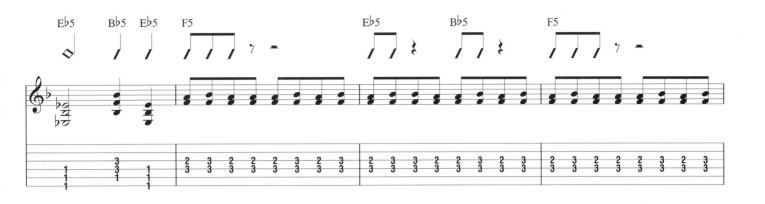

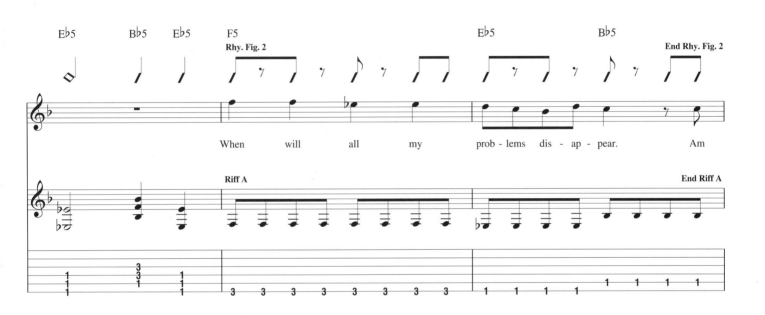

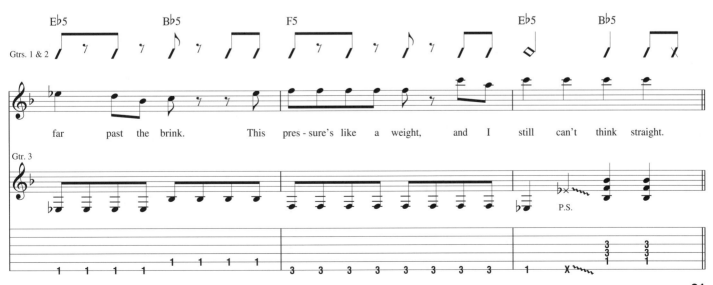

a - bout? All these ag - gra - va - tions,_____

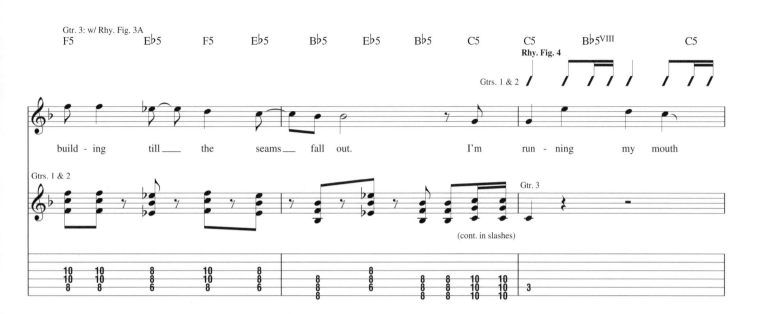

Gtr. 3: w/ Rhy. Fig. 3A

Rhy. Fig. 4

Gtrs. 1 & 2

build - ing till ___ the seams ___ fall out. I'm run - ning my mouth

Gtrs. 1 & 2

Gtr. 3

(cont. in slashes)

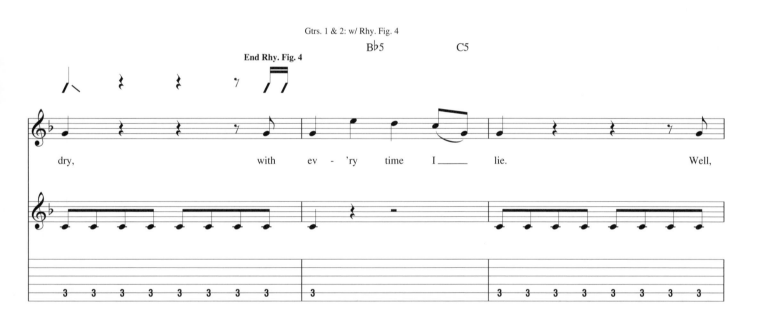

Gtrs. 1 & 2: w/ Rhy. Fig. 4

End Rhy. Fig. 4

dry, with ev - 'ry time I ___ lie. Well,

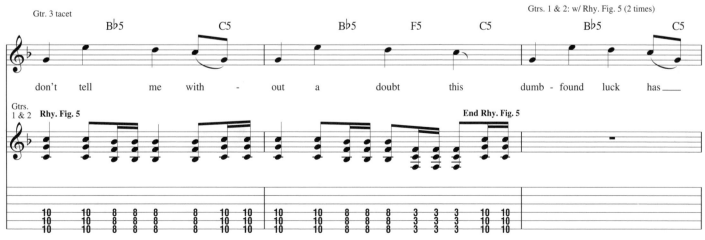

Gtr. 3 tacet

Gtrs. 1 & 2: w/ Rhy. Fig. 5 (2 times)

don't tell me with - out a doubt this dumb - found luck has ___

Gtrs. 1 & 2 Rhy. Fig. 5

End Rhy. Fig. 5

all   run   out.   All   out.

Don't   tell   me   with   -   out   a   doubt   this

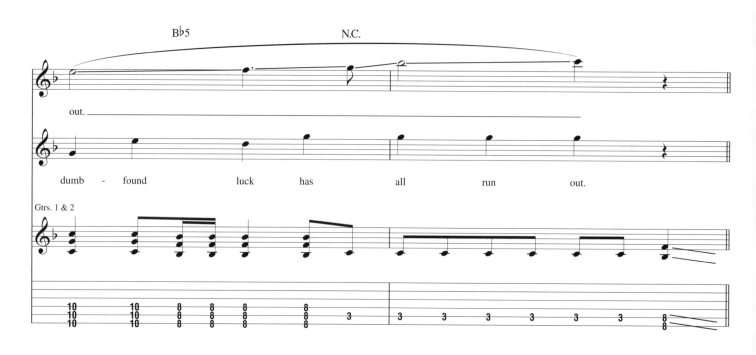

out.

dumb   -   found   luck   has   all   run   out.

Gtrs. 1 & 2

Chorus

Gtrs. 1 & 2: w/ Rhy. Fig. 1 (1 1/2 times)

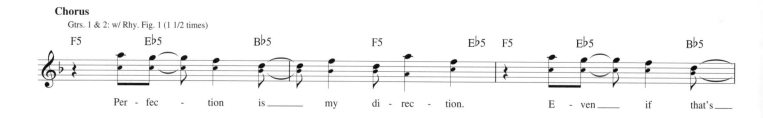

Per   -   fec   -   tion   is   my   di   -   rec   -   tion.   E   -   ven   if   that's

    all   I   had.   It's   not   like   I   need   no   cor   -   rec   -   tion.

I   just   know   that   life's   not   so   bad.

Gtrs. 1 & 2

Still Waiting

Words and Music by Sum 41 and Greig Andrew Nori

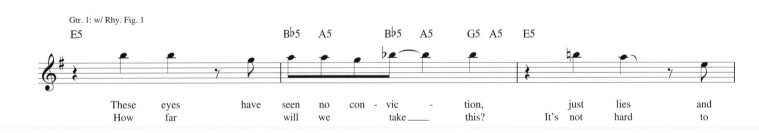

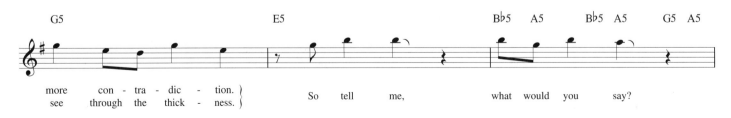

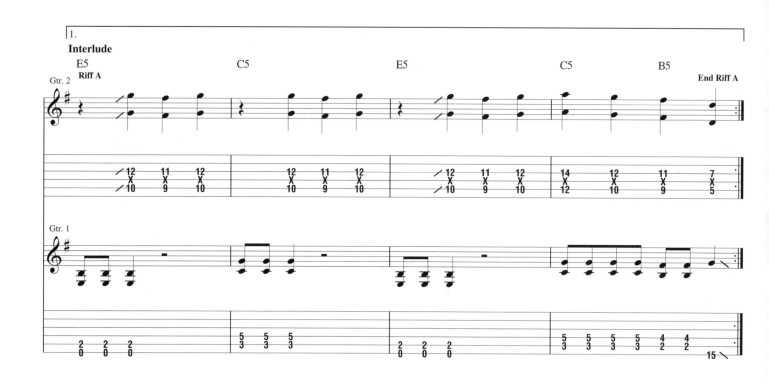

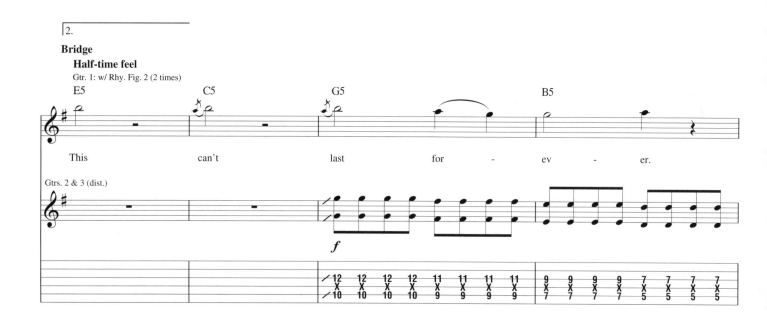

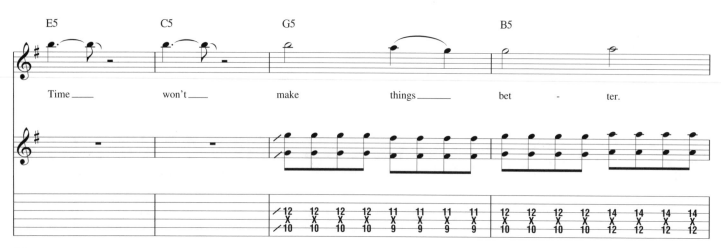

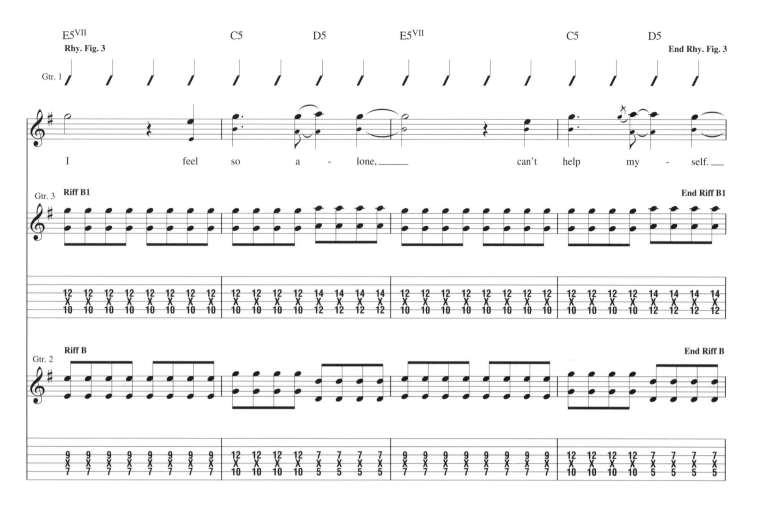

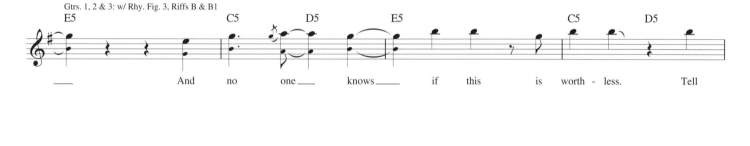

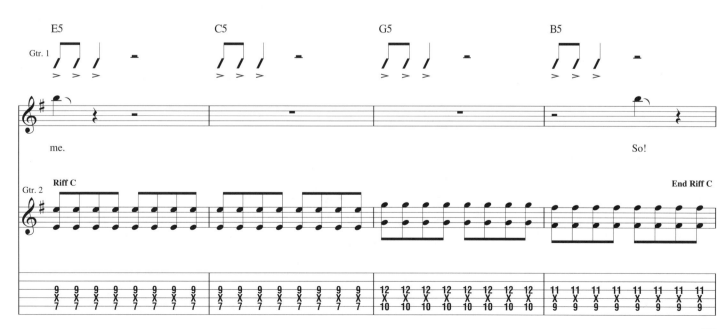

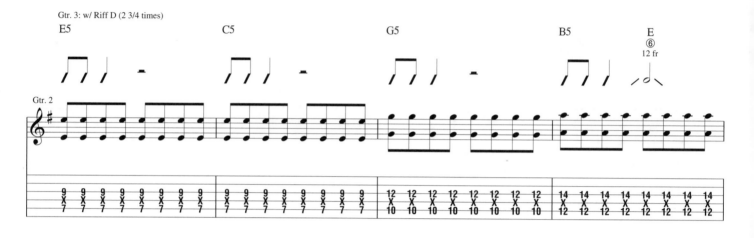

What have ___ we done with a war that can't be won? This can't

be real. I don't know what to feel. _____

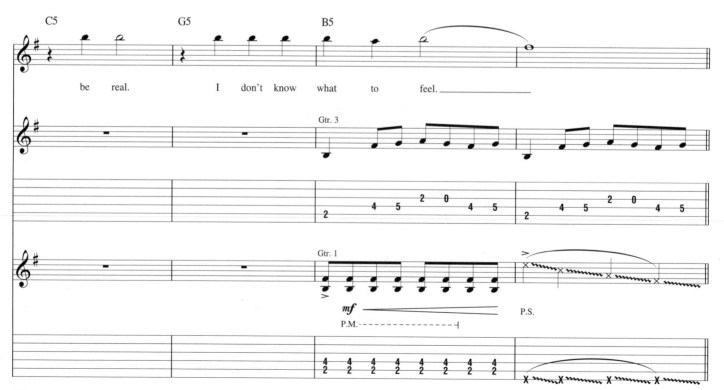

Gtr. 1: w/ Rhy. Fig. 2 (4 times)
Gtr. 2: w/ Riff A (2 times)

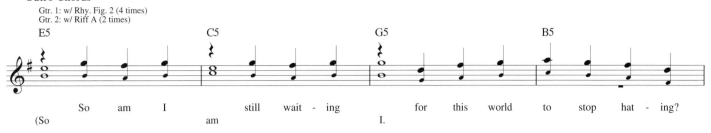

So am I still wait - ing for this world to stop hat - ing?
(So am I.

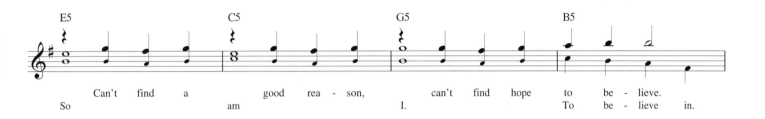

Can't find a good rea - son, can't find hope to be - lieve.
So am I. To be - lieve in.

Gtr. 3: w/ Riff D (2 times)

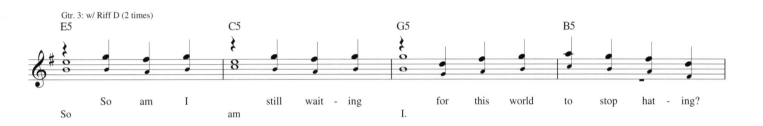

So am I still wait - ing for this world to stop hat - ing?
So am I.

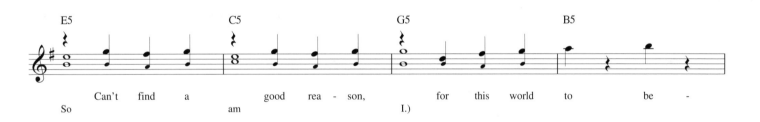

Can't find a good rea - son, for this world to be -
So am I.)

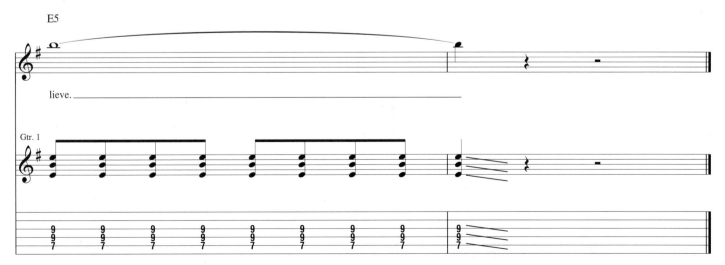

lieve. _____

Gtr. 1

A.N.I.C.
Words and Music by Sum 41 and Greig Andrew Nori

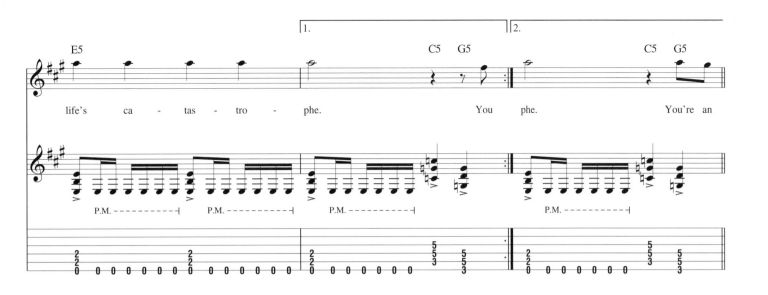

life's ca- tas- tro- phe.   You phe.   You're an

Chorus

Gtrs. 1 & 2: w/ Rhy. Fig. 1 (1 3/4 times)

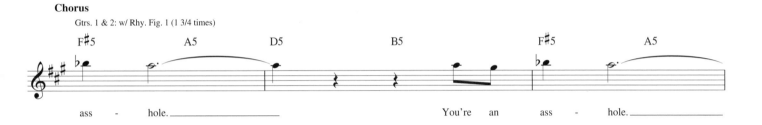

ass- hole._____   You're an   ass- hole._____

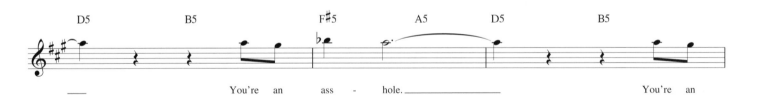

_____   You're an   ass- hole._____   You're an

Free time

Gtr. 2 tacet

ass- hole._____   You make me sick.

*w/ Digitech Whammy Pedal

*Set for two octaves above.

No Brains

Words and Music by Sum 41 and Greig Andrew Nori

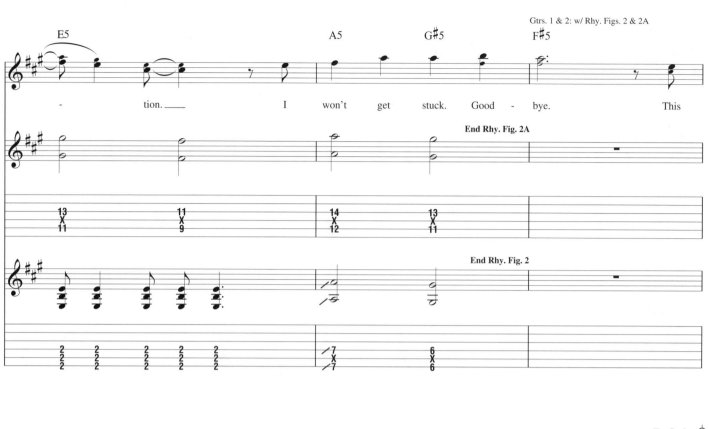

-tion. ___ I won't get stuck. Good - bye. This

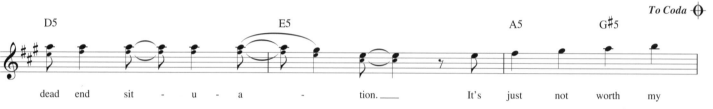

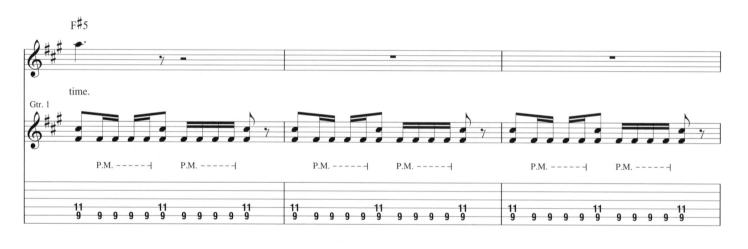

dead end sit - u - a - tion. ___ It's just not worth my

time.

2. It's no bet - ter to - day. ___

All Messed Up

Words and Music by Sum 41 and Greig Andrew Nori

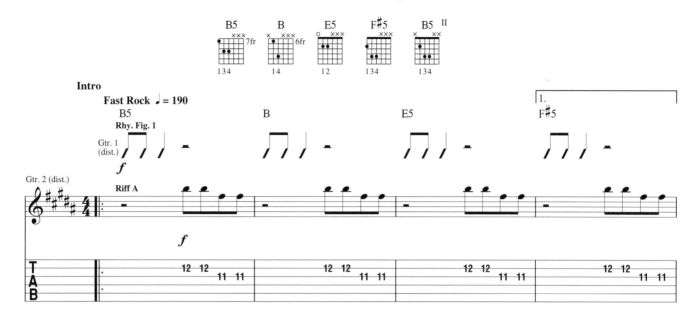

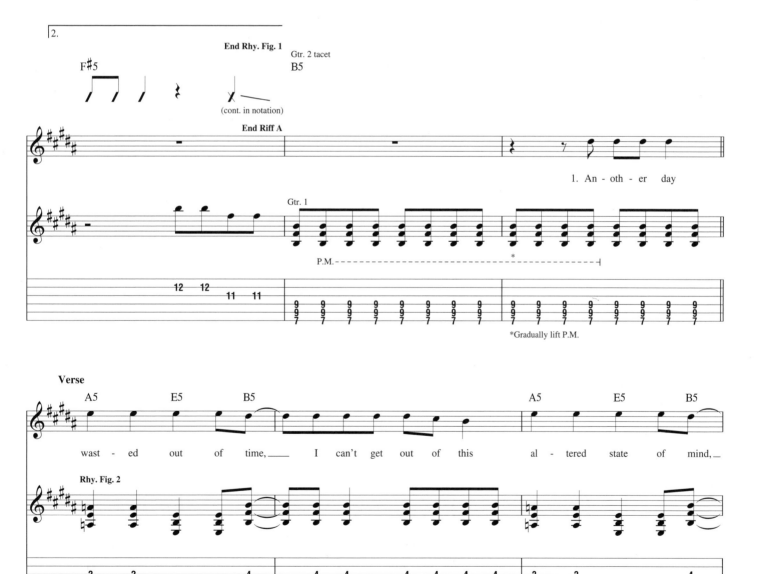

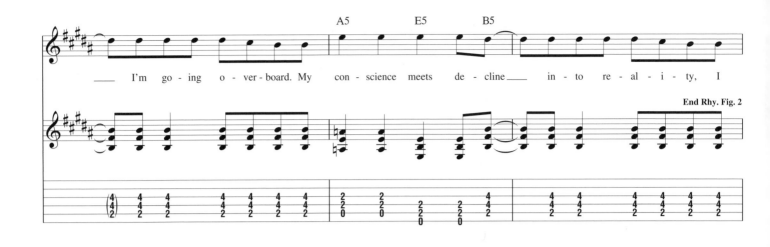

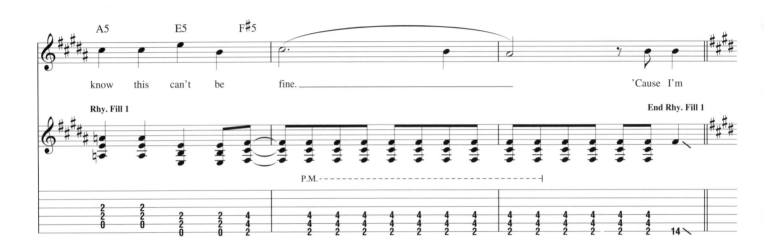

$\mathsection$ **Chorus**

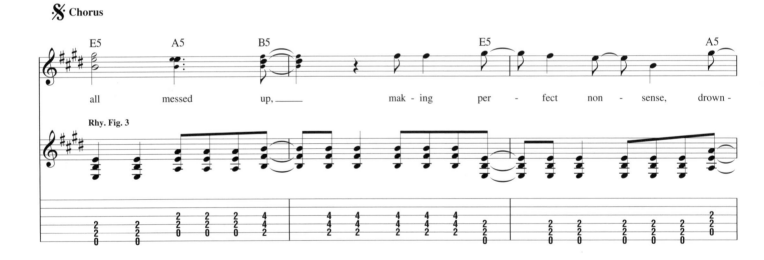

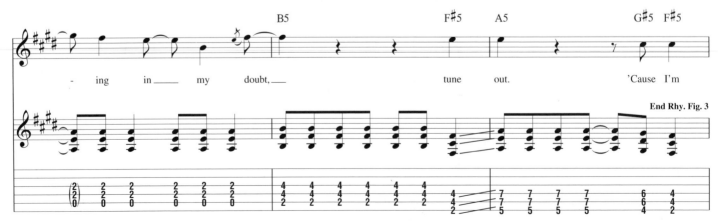

all messed up, _____ go - ing no - where fast _____ but cir -

To Coda 1 ⊕   *To Coda 2* ⊕

- cles in _____ my mind, _____ so blind.

Interlude

2. Who are these

Verse

Gtr. 1: w/ Rhy. Fig. 4 (2 times)

voic - es in my head? ____ I can't go on like this, liv - ing like the dead, ____

_____ I have - n't slept so long. Feel - ing sad, I dread,_____ I'm talk - ing to my - self, for -

D.S. al Coda 1

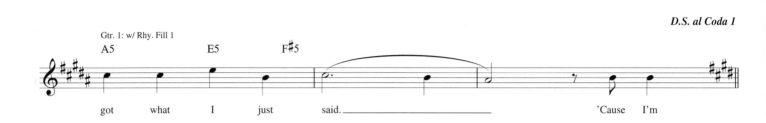

Gtr. 1: w/ Rhy. Fill 1

got what I just said._____ 'Cause I'm

⊕ Coda 1

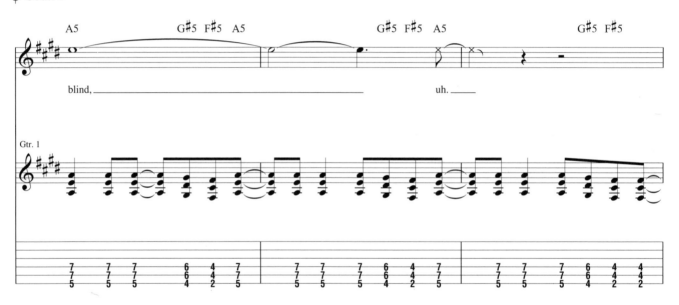

blind,_____ uh._____

Bridge

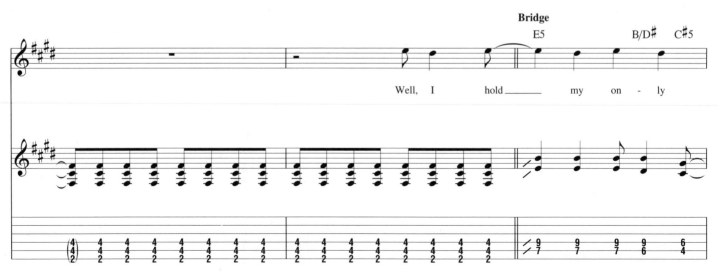

Well, I hold_____ my on - ly

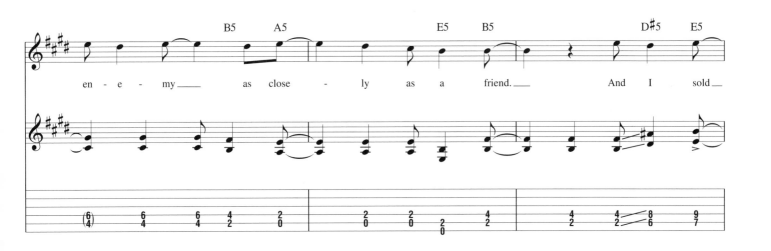

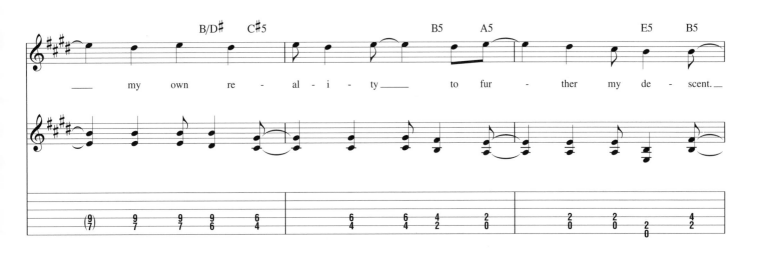

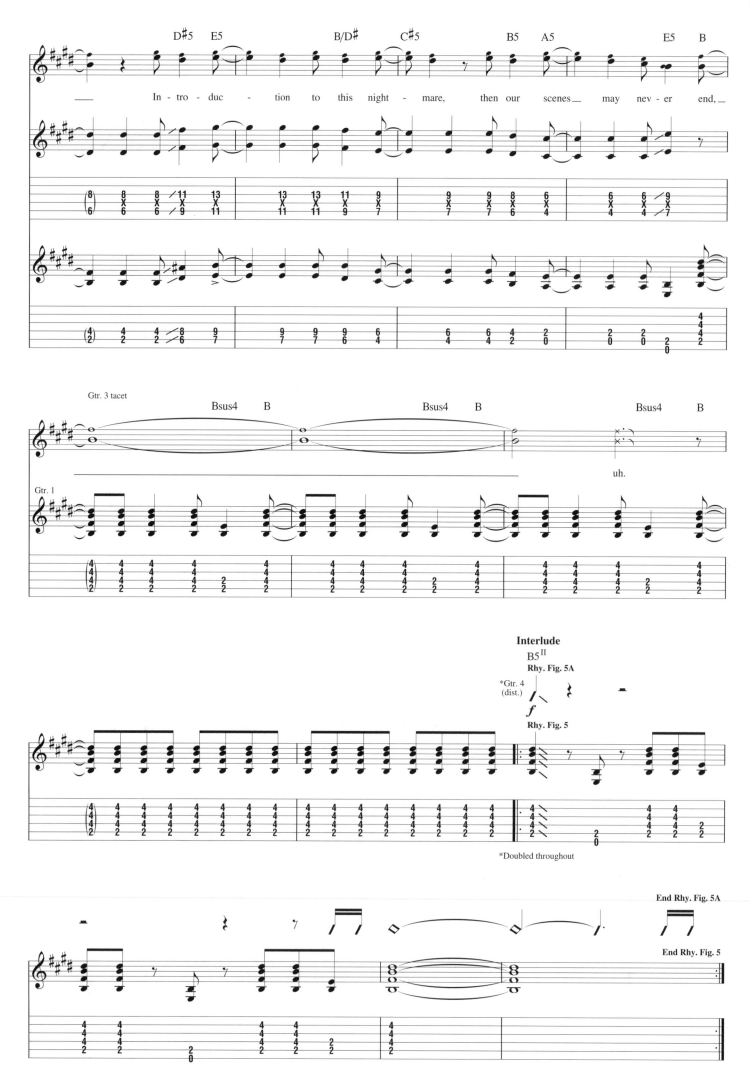

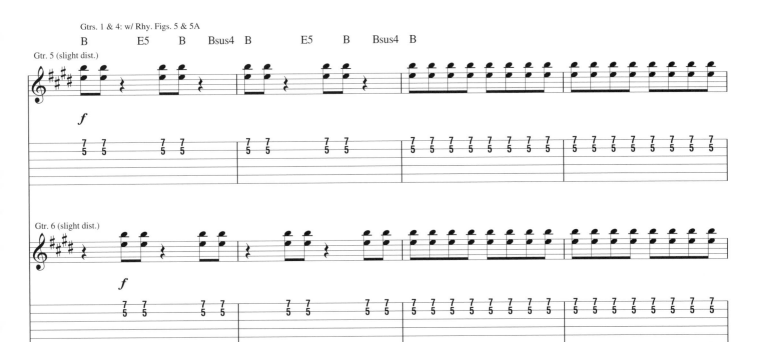

Verse

Gtr. 1: w/ Rhy. Fig. 2
Gtrs. 4, 5 & 6 tacet

help me drag my heels?___ I'm run-ning o-ver-time I can't hold down my meals,___

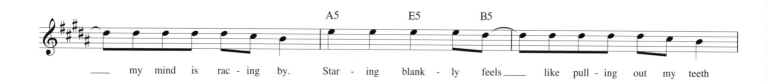

___ my mind is rac-ing by. Star-ing blank-ly feels___ like pull-ing out my teeth

D.S. al Coda 2

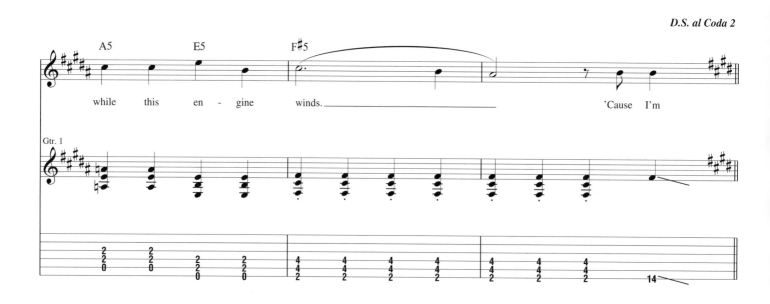

while this en-gine winds._____ 'Cause I'm

Gtr. 1

⊕ Coda 2

Outro

Gtr. 1: w/ Rhy. Fig. 1
Gtr. 2: w/ Riff A

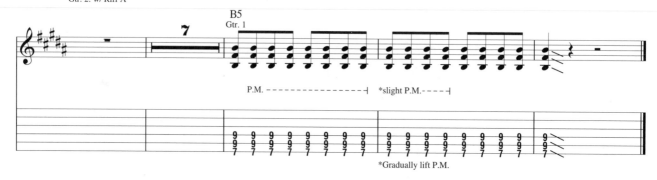

Mr. Amsterdam

Words and Music by Sum 41 and Greig Andrew Nori

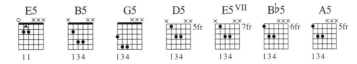

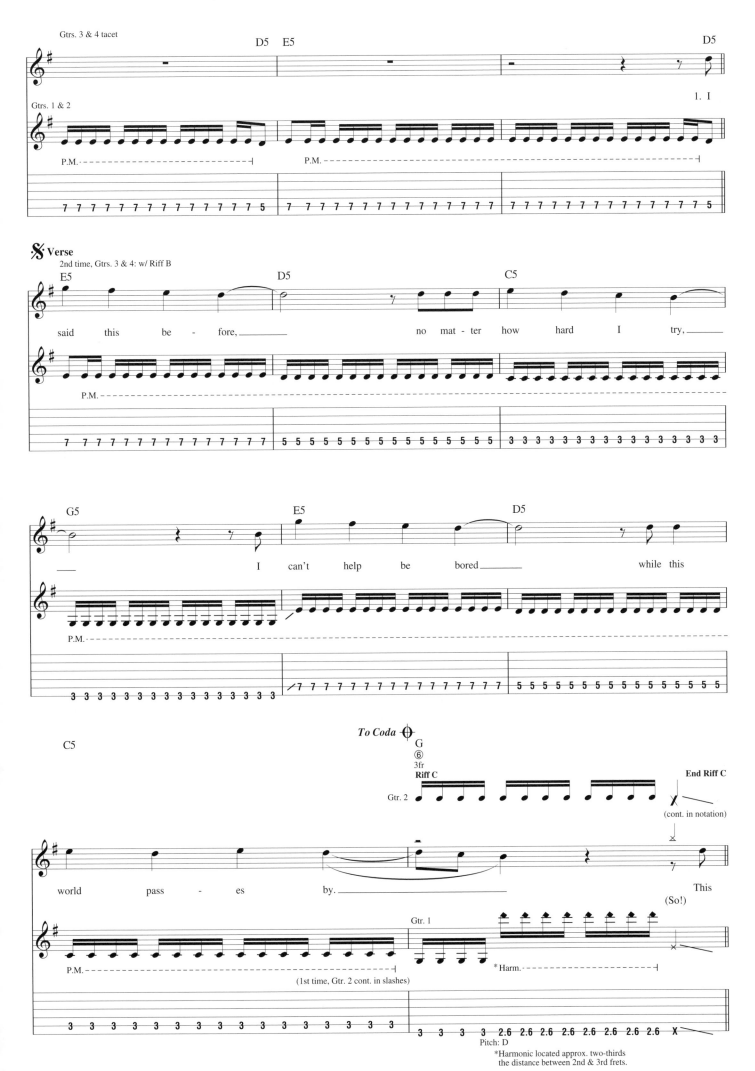

rev - e - la - tion's got no mean - ing, we lost it all ___ in hope -

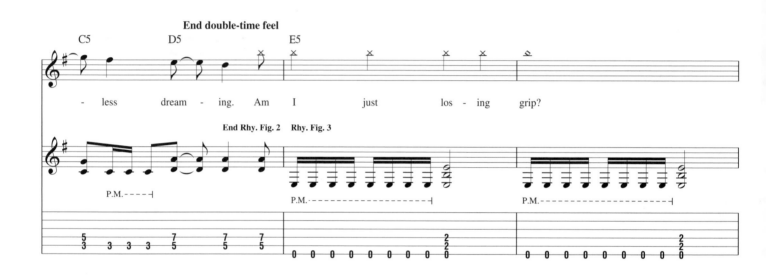

- less dream - ing. Am I just los - ing grip?

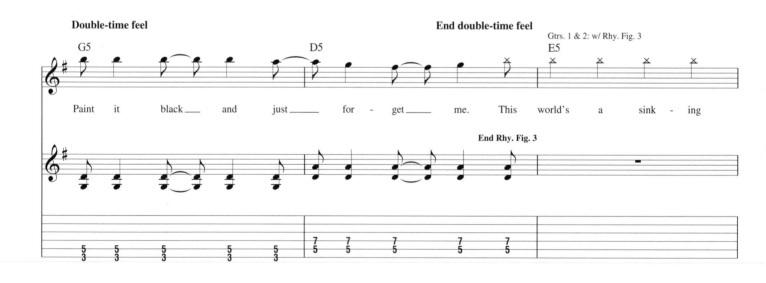

Paint it black ___ and just ___ for - get ___ me. This world's a sink - ing

ship! 'Cause our bag - gage is ___ too heav - y.

Chorus
Gtrs. 1 & 2: w/ Rhy. Fig. 2 (2 times)

I can't stop be-liev-ing there's some-thing to be said. What are we a-chiev-ing with the

bull-shit that we're fed? I know I'm not gon-na stay or live to see the day this

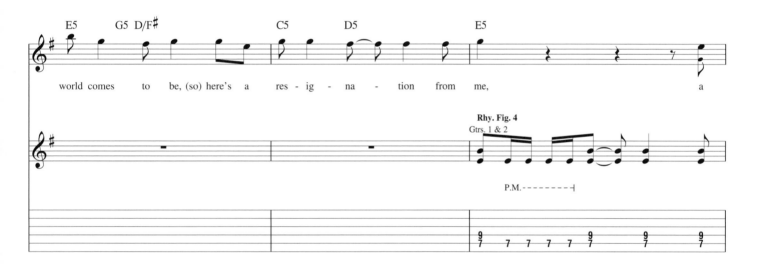

world comes to be, (so) here's a res-ig-na-tion from me, a

Rhy. Fig. 4
Gtrs. 1 & 2

P.M.----------┤

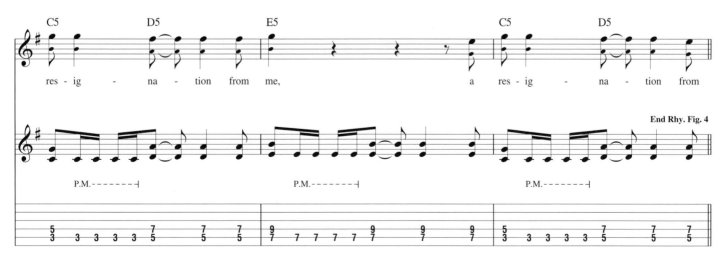

res-ig-na-tion from me, a res-ig-na-tion from

End Rhy. Fig. 4

P.M.-------┤   P.M.-------┤   P.M.-------┤

55

Interlude

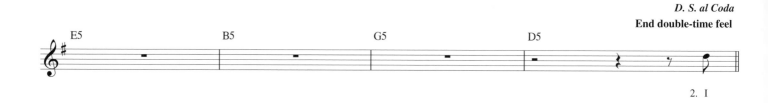

Coda

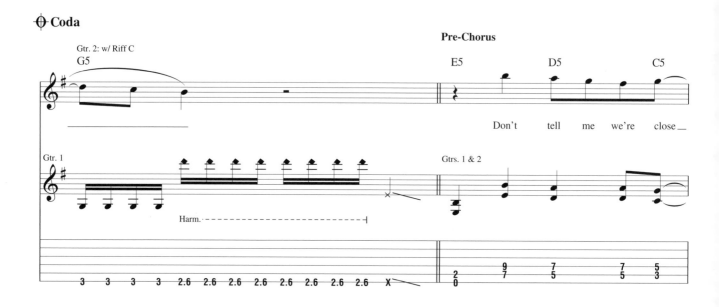

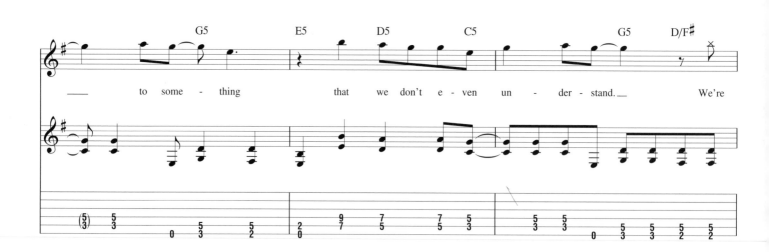

Double-time feel

out - side's all I know! I'm the one ___ here to ___ com - plain. ___

Chorus

Gtrs. 1 & 2: w/ Rhy. Fig. 2

I can't find the an - swers to save hu - man - i - ty. I can't fight the an - ger, here's a res - ig - na - tion from

Gtrs. 1 & 2: w/ Rhy. Fig. 4 (2 times)

me, a res - ig - na - tion from me, a res - ig - na - tion from

End double-time feel

me, a res - ig - na - tion from me, a res - ig - na - tion from

Interlude

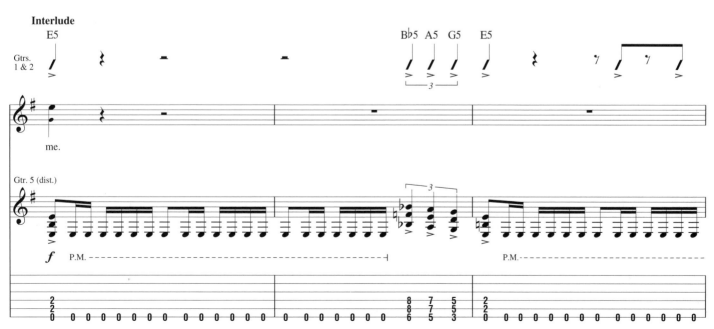

me.

Gtr. 5 (dist.)

f P.M. - P.M. - - - - - - - - - - - - - - - -

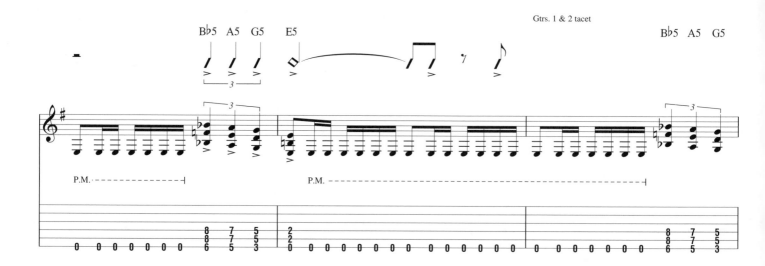

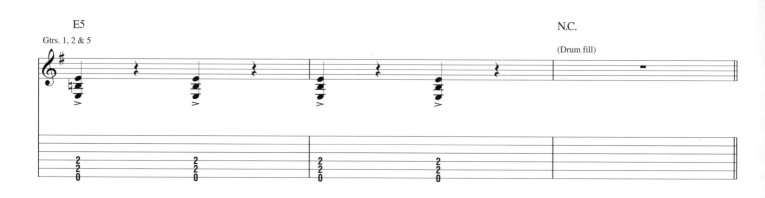

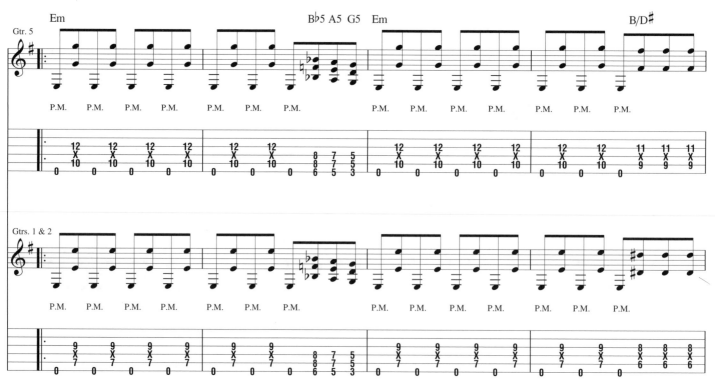

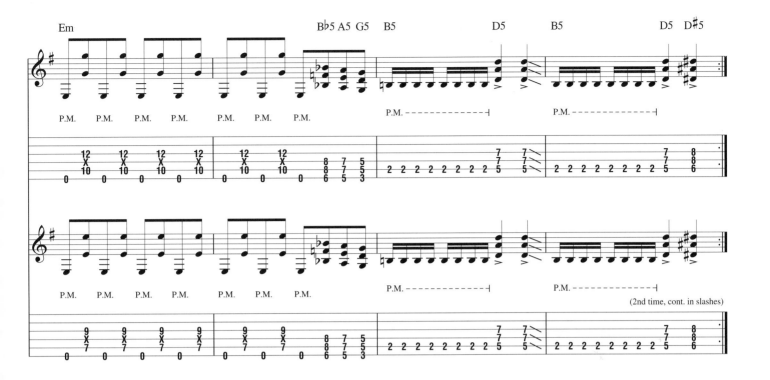

Outro
Double-time feel

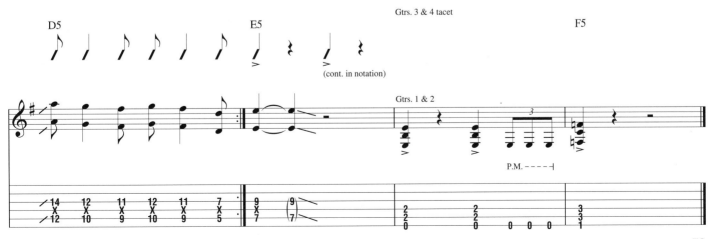

Thanks for Nothing

Words and Music by Sum 41 and Greig Andrew Nori

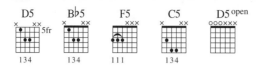

Drop D tuning:
(low to high) D-A-D-G-B-E

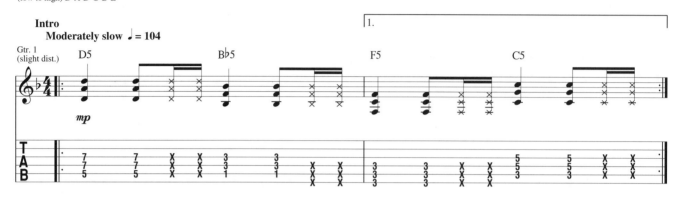

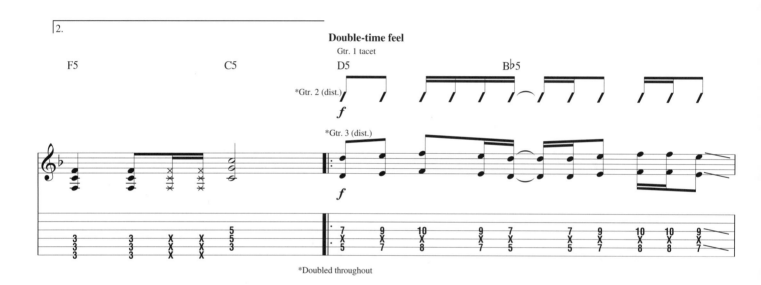

*Doubled throughout

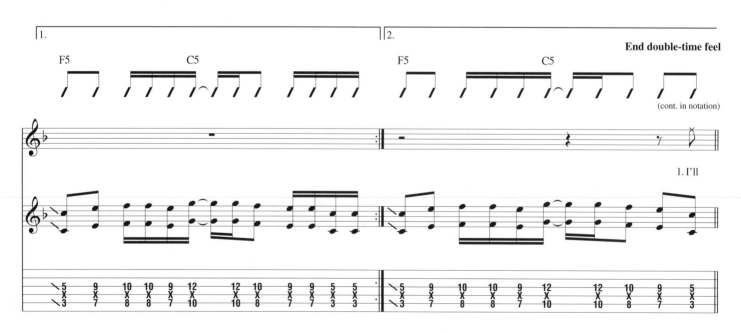

Verse

D5   B♭5   Gtr. 3 tacet   F5   C5

nev - er take part in the grow-ing pop - u - la - tion or waste my time with fur - ther ed - u - ca - tion. For-
can't take part in the busi-ness-man il - lu - sion, I'll take my chance in the real world con - fu - sion.

(Ah.   Hoo,   ha!)

Gtr. 3

Gtr. 2

P.M. ⌐

D5   B♭5   F5   C5

get what we know, it's just a big show what they want to con - trol. So
Don't blame us, who do we trust when they're so dis - hon - est? No

Gtr. 2

P.M. ⌐

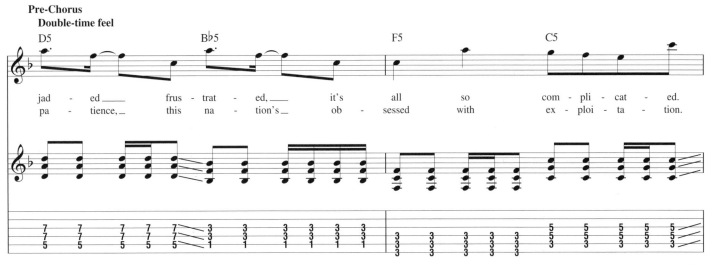

Pre-Chorus
Double-time feel

D5   B♭5   F5   C5

jad - ed frus - trat - ed, it's all so com - pli - cat - ed.
pa - tience, this na - tion's ob - sessed with ex - ploi - ta - tion.

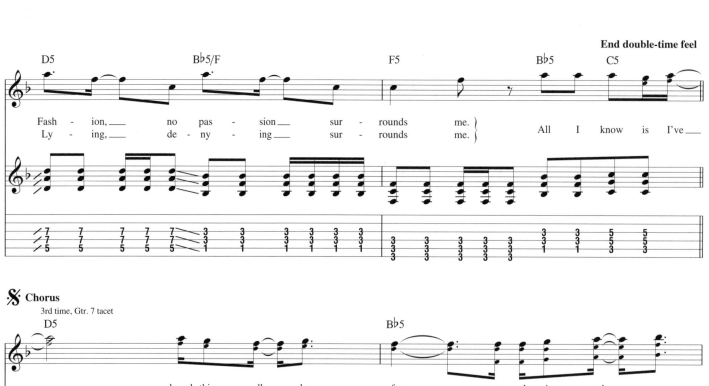

Chorus
3rd time, Gtr. 7 tacet

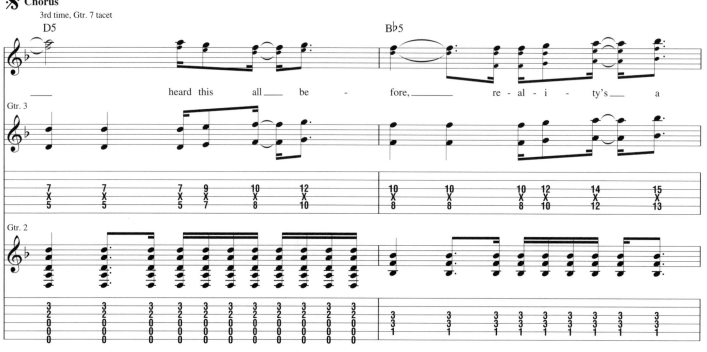

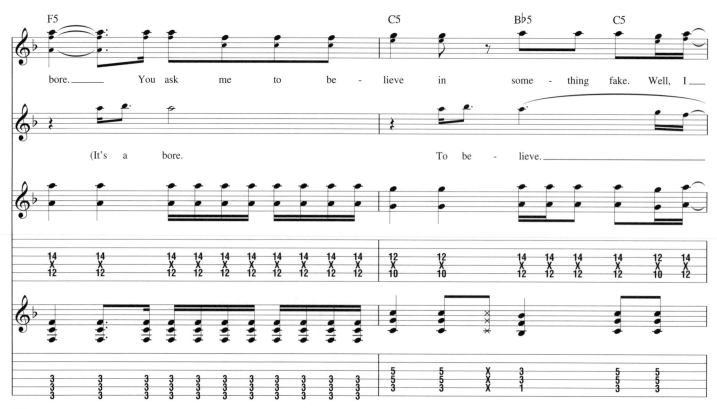

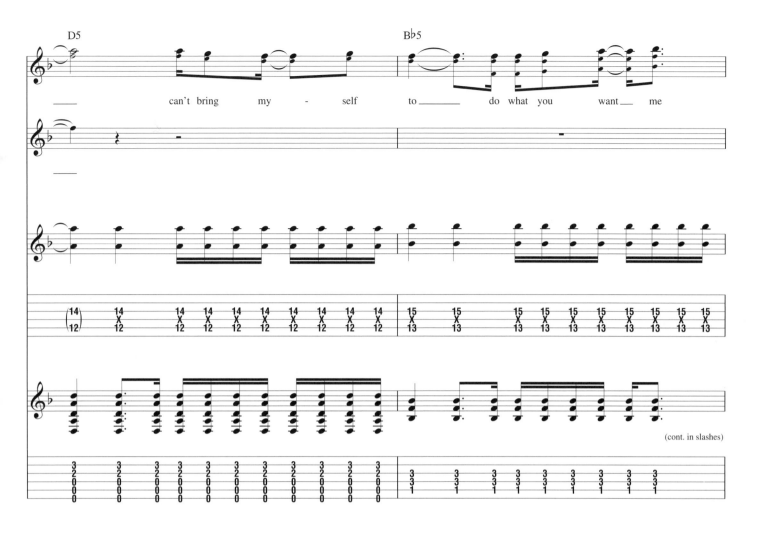

can't bring my - self to _____ do what you want _____ me

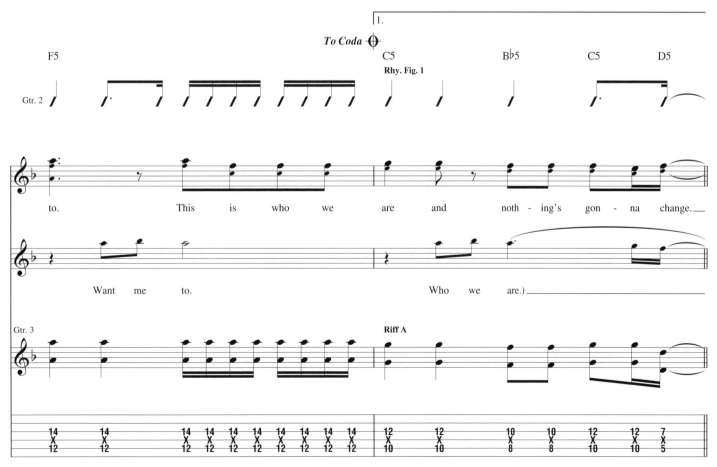

to. This is who we are and noth - ing's gon - na change. _____

Want me to. Who we are.) _____

Interlude

Double-time feel

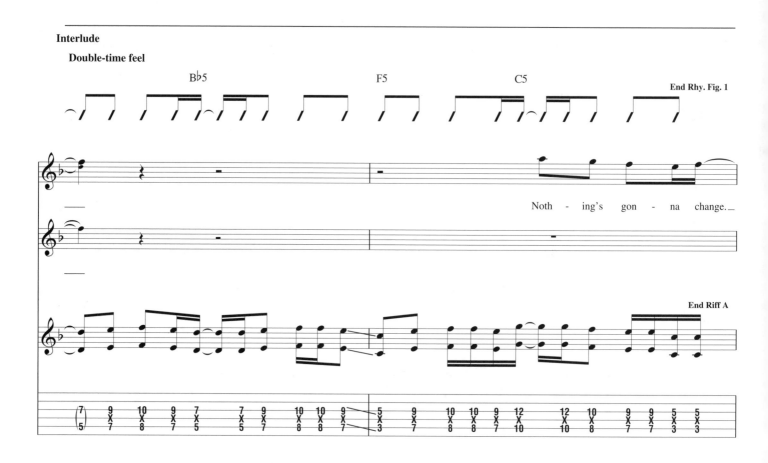

Noth - ing's gon - na change.

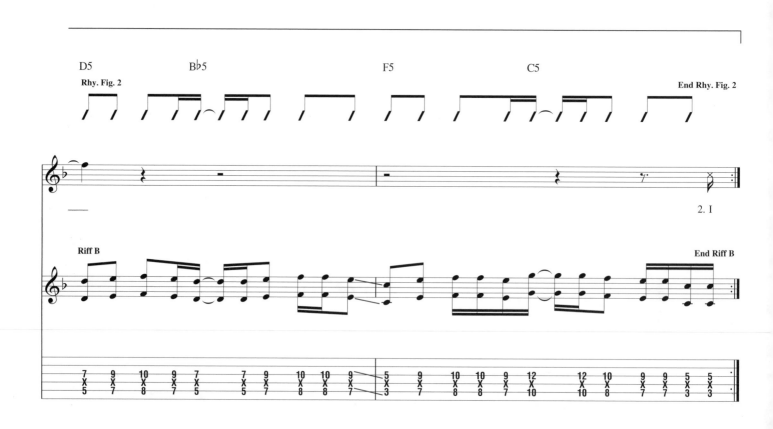

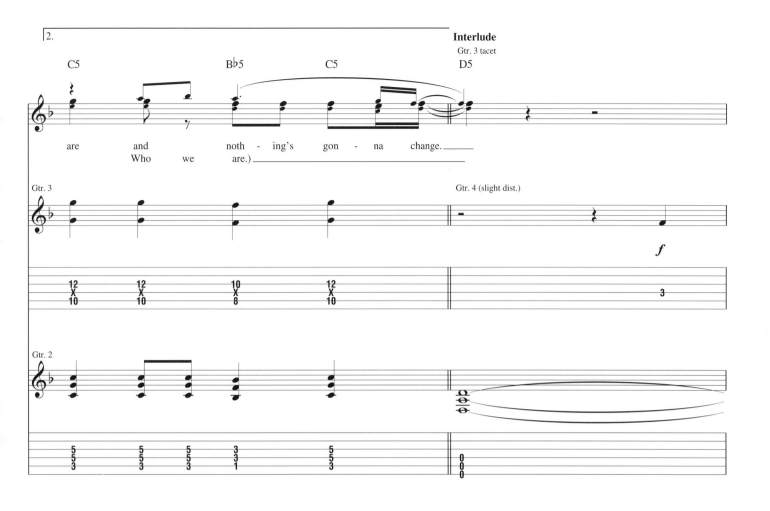

*Doubled throughout

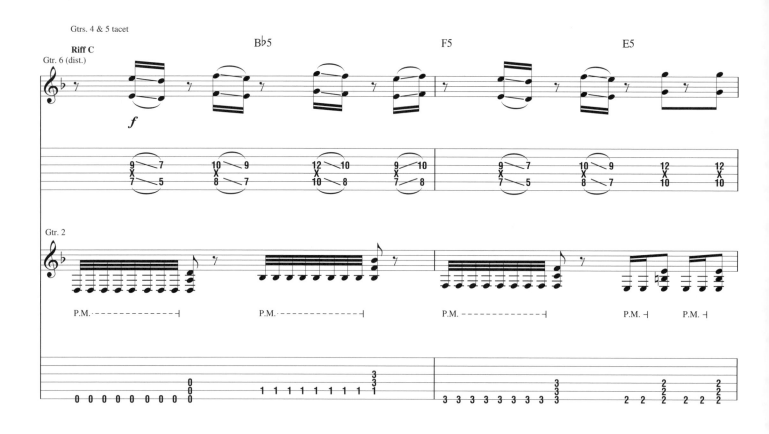

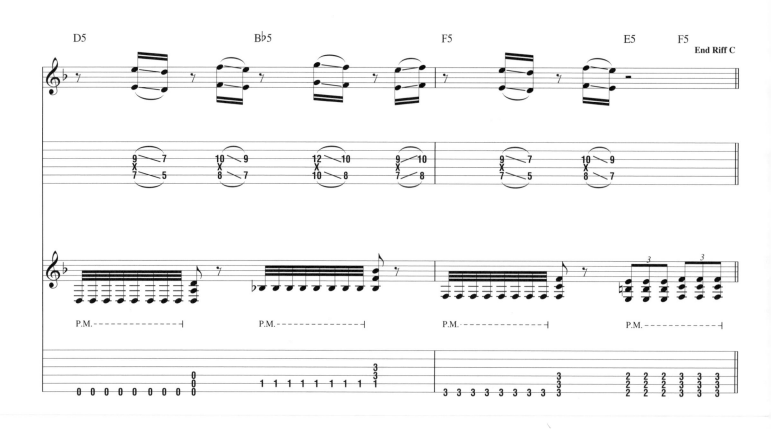

Bridge

Gtr. 6: w/ Riff C

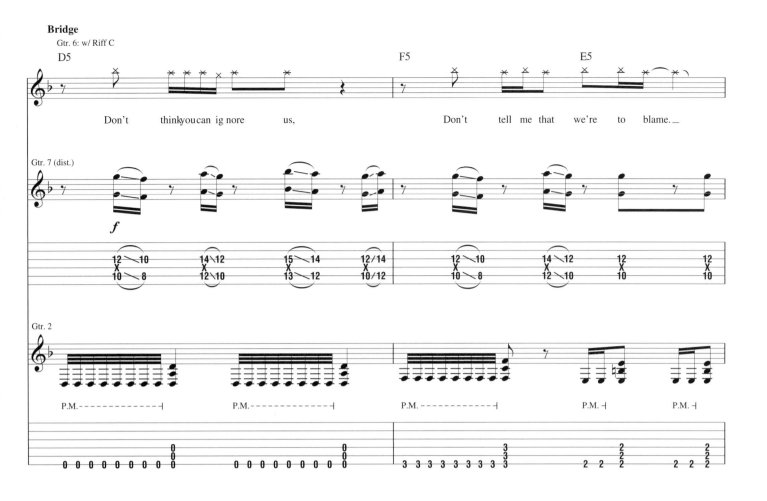

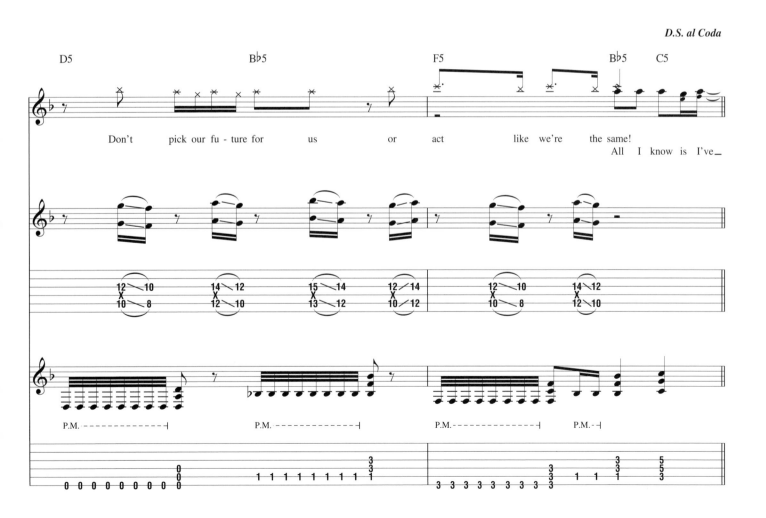

Coda

Outro
Double-time feel

Gtr. 2: w/ Rhy. Fig. 1
Gtr. 3: w/ Riff A

C5   Bb5   C5   D5   Bb5   F5   C5

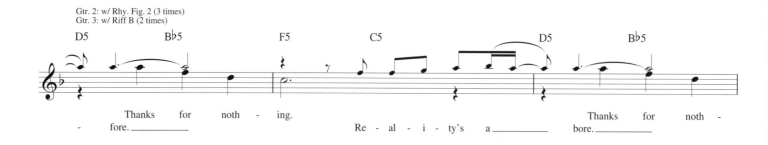

are and noth-ing's gon-na change.___ Thanks for noth - ing.
Who we are.)_____ (I've heard this all be -

Gtr. 2: w/ Rhy. Fig. 2 (3 times)
Gtr. 3: w/ Riff B (2 times)

D5   Bb5   F5   C5   D5   Bb5

Thanks for noth - ing.
- fore._____ Re - al - i - ty's a ___ bore._____ Thanks for noth -

F5   C5   D   Bb5

ing.
It - 'll nev - er be the ___ same. Thanks for noth -

Gtr. 3

```
7   9   10  9   7       7   9   10  10  9
X   X   X   X   X       X   X   X   X   X
5   7   8   7   5       5   7   8   8   7
```

Segue to "Hyper-
Insomnia-Para-Condrioid"

Free time

F5   C5   D5 open

Gtr. 2

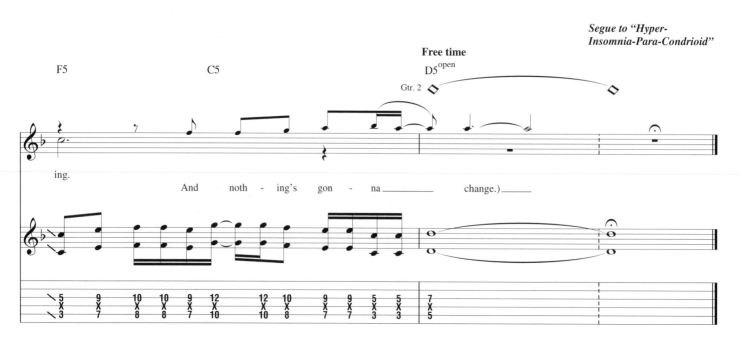

ing.
And noth - ing's gon - na ___ change.)___

```
5   9   10  10  9   12      12  10  9   9   5   5       7
X   X   X   X   X   X       X   X   X   X   X   X       X
3   7   8   8   7   10      10  8   7   7   3   3       5
```

Hyper-Insomnia-Para-Condrioid

Words and Music by Sum 41 and Greig Andrew Nori

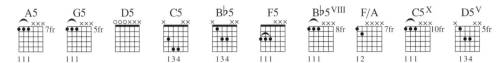

Drop D tuning:
(low to high) D-A-D-G-B-E

Intro

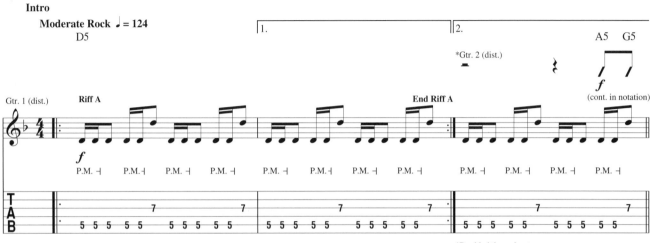

*Doubled throughout

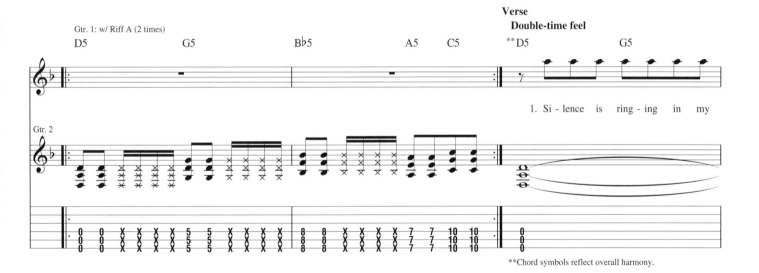

**Chord symbols reflect overall harmony.

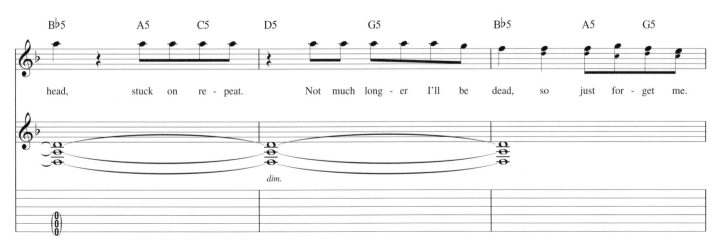

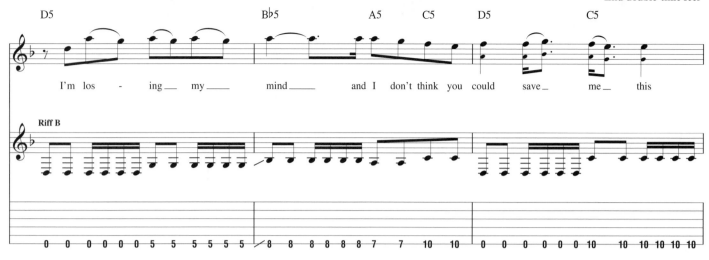

I'm los - ing ___ my ___ mind ___ and I don't think you could save ___ me ___ this

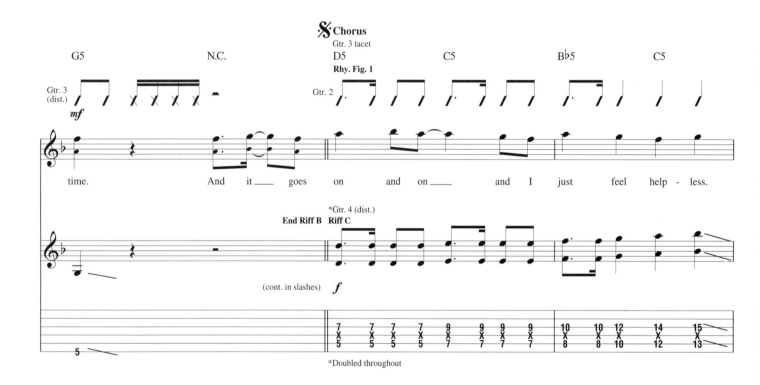

time. And it ___ goes on and on ___ and I just feel help - less.

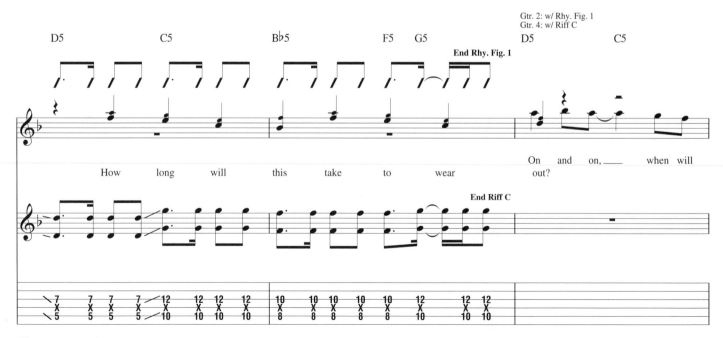

How long will this take to wear out? On and on, ___ when will

⊕ Coda 1

Bridge

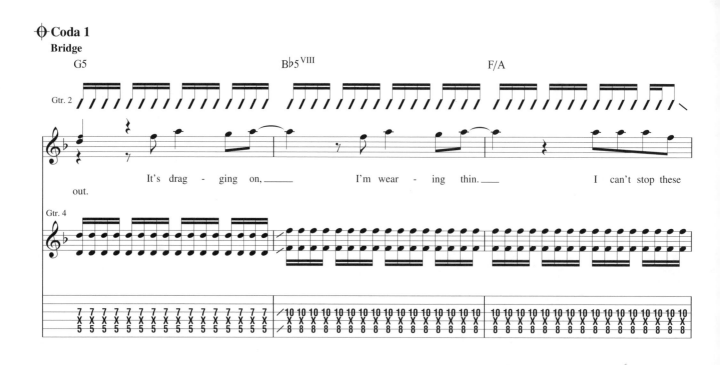

It's drag - ging on, _____ I'm wear - ing thin. _____ I can't stop these
out.

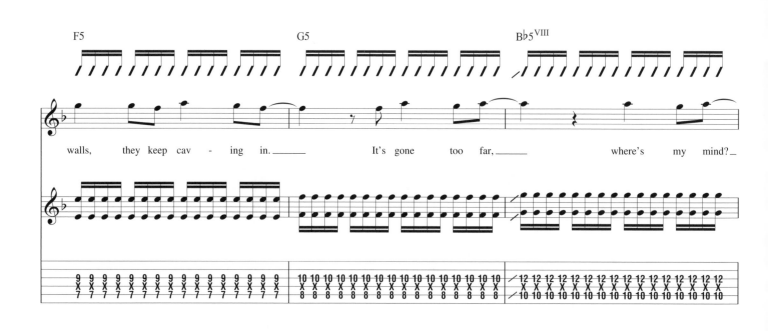

walls, they keep cav - ing in. _____ It's gone too far, _____ where's my mind?

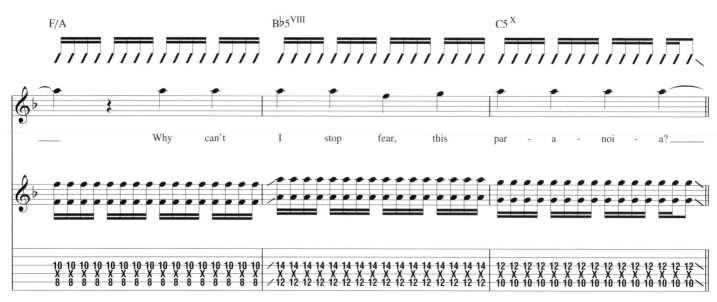

Why can't I stop fear, this par - a - noi - a? _____

Interlude

D5

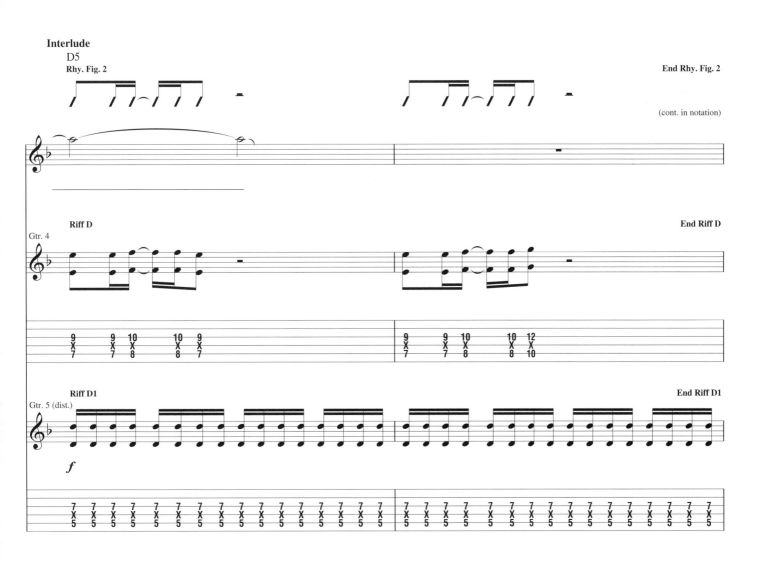

Gtrs. 4 & 5: w/ Riffs D & D1 (2 1/2 times)

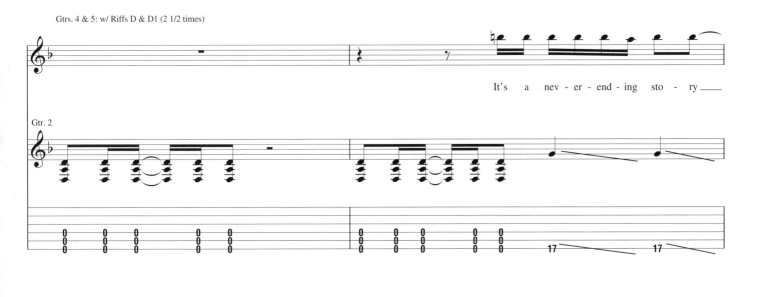

It's a nev-er-end-ing sto-ry___

Gtr. 2: w/ Rhy. Fig. 2 (1 1/2 times)

___ and it starts with me!   It's a nev-er-end-ing sto-ry___   and it starts   with

Billy Spleen

Words and Music by Sum 41 and Greig Andrew Nori

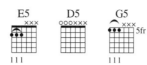

Drop D tuning:
(low to high) D-A-D-G-B-E

* Intro
Free time (♩ = 120)

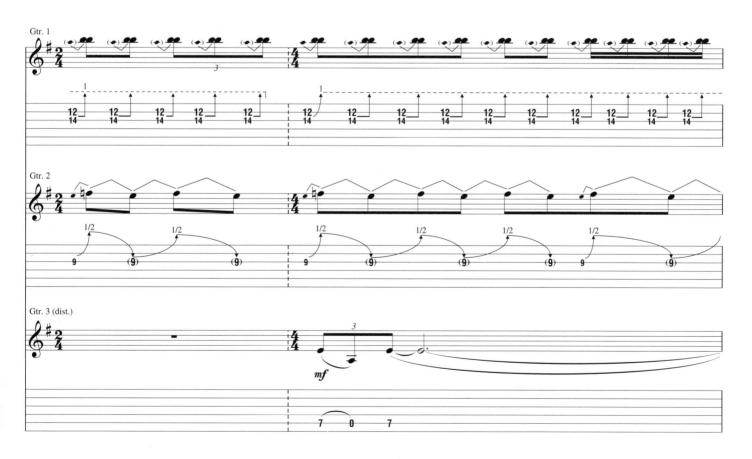

*Song begins at 2:32 of previous track.

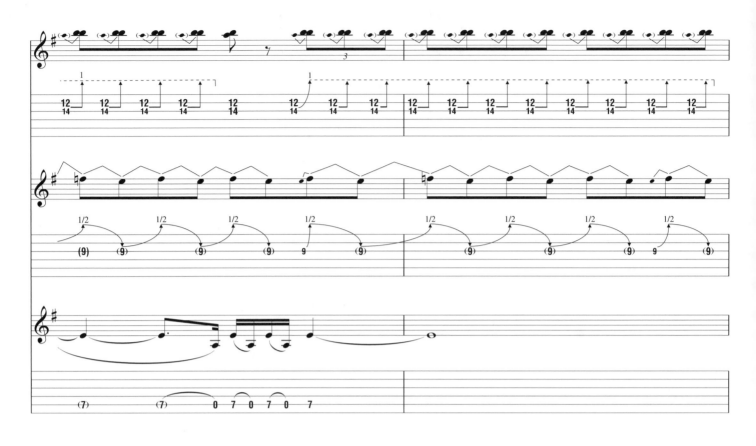

Moderately fast ♩ = 120
Double-time feel

Gtrs. 1, 2 & 3 tacet

E5

Rhy. Fig. 1

*Gtr. 4
(dist.)

f

*Gtr. 5 (dist.)

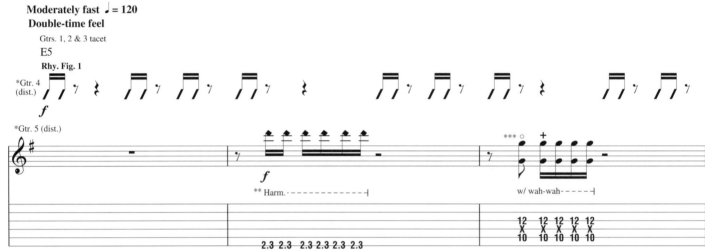

*** o   +

** Harm. - - - - - - - - - - - - ⌐

w/ wah-wah - - - - - ⌐

*Doubled throughout

Pitch: D

**Harmonic located approx. one-third the distance between 2nd & 3rd frets.

***Wah-wah indications: o = open (toe up);
+ = closed (toe down)

End double-time feel

Gtr. 5 tacet

End Rhy. Fig. 1

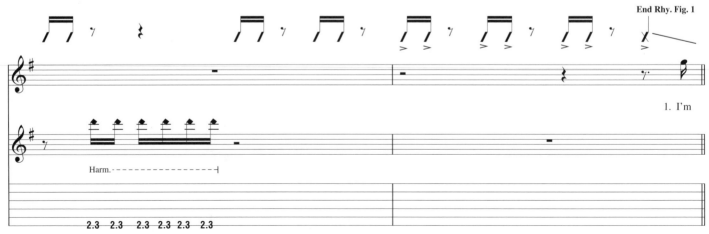

1. I'm

Harm. - - - - - - - - - - - - ⌐

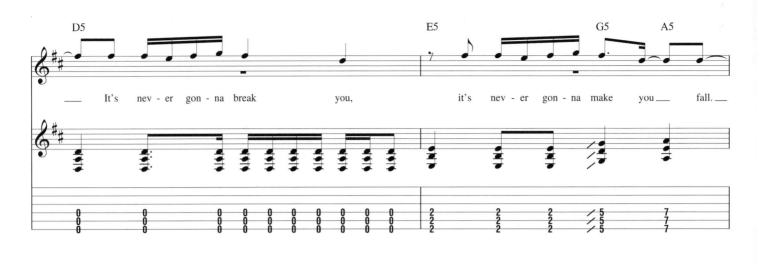

It's nev-er gon-na break you, it's nev-er gon-na make you fall.

To Coda ⊕

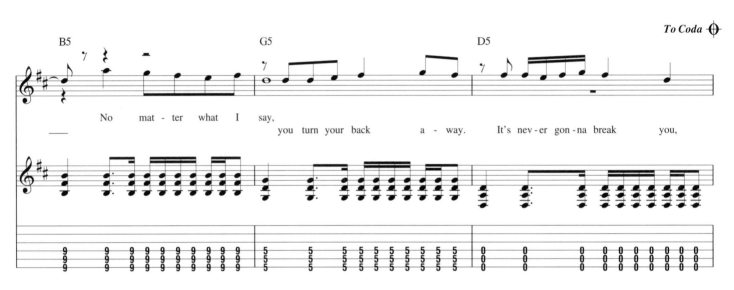

No mat-ter what I say, you turn your back a-way. It's nev-er gon-na break you,

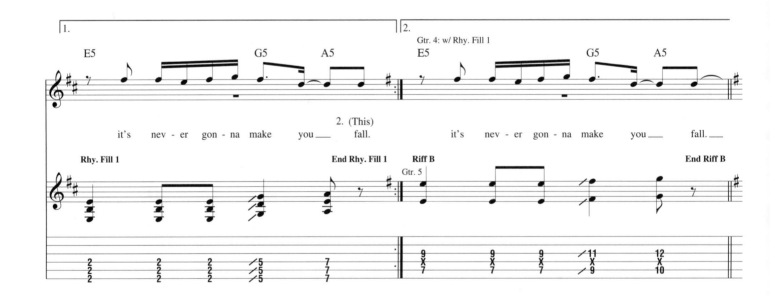

1.

it's nev-er gon-na make you fall.

2. (This)

it's nev-er gon-na make you fall.

Gtr. 4: w/ Rhy. Fill 1

Rhy. Fill 1   End Rhy. Fill 1   Riff B   End Riff B

Gtr. 5

Bridge
Double-time feel

Gtr. 4: w/ Rhy. Fig. 1
Gtr. 5 tacet

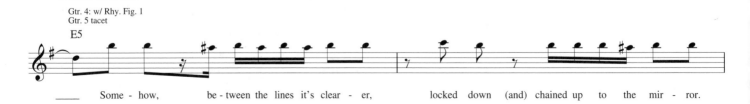

Some - how, be - tween the lines it's clear - er, locked down (and) chained up to the mir - ror.

End double-time feel

Some-how,   be-tween the lines it's clear-er.   Locked down,   it takes   a   part   of   me.   What's up?

Interlude

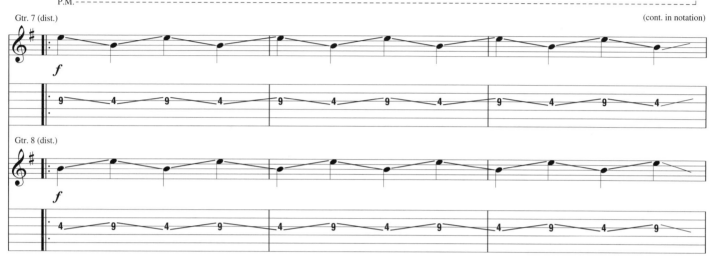

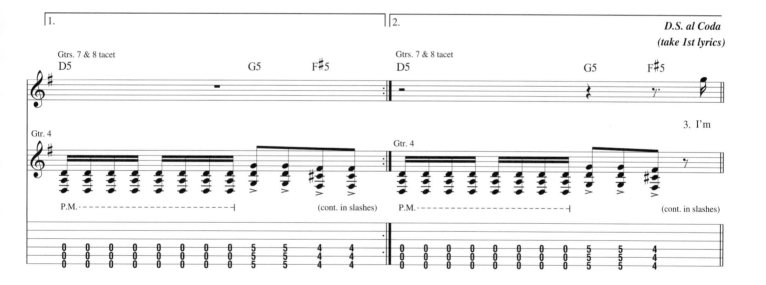

3. I'm

Coda

Gtr. 4: w/ Rhy. Fill 1
Gtr. 5: w/ Riff B

it's   nev-er   gon-na   make   you ____   fall. ____

Additional Lyrics

2. (This) fake reality,
(I) never can make up the time that you're taking.
It's my worst enemy.
I'm on a mission to feed my addiction.
So sick of thoughts so empty.
It's well overflowed, I'm bound to explode.
So much, so much for what, for what we said.

(To Chorus)

79

Hooch

Words and Music by Sum 41 and Greig Andrew Nori

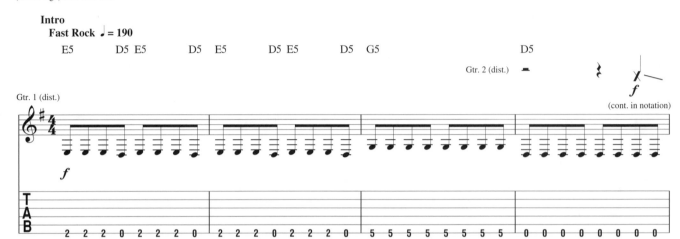

Drop D tuning:
(low to high) D-A-D-G-B-E

Intro
Fast Rock ♩ = 190

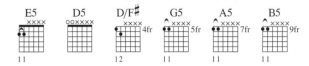

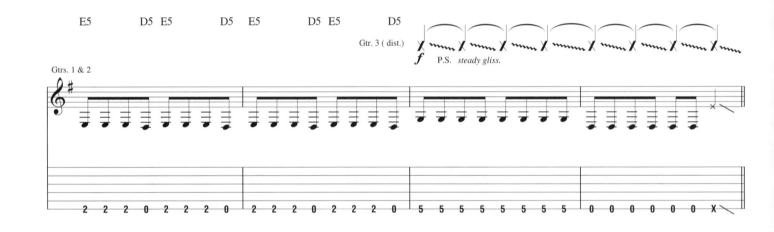

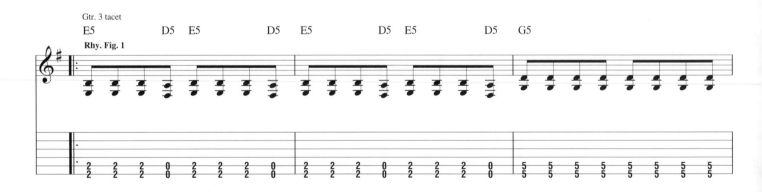

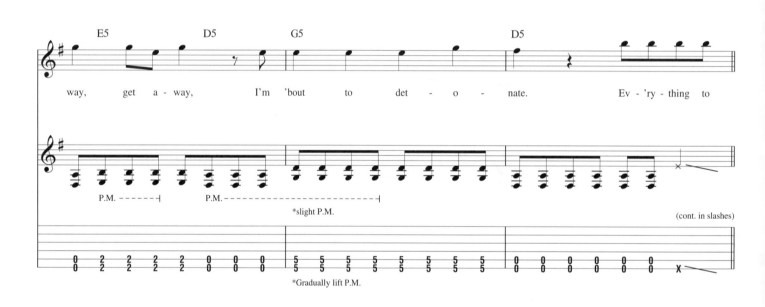

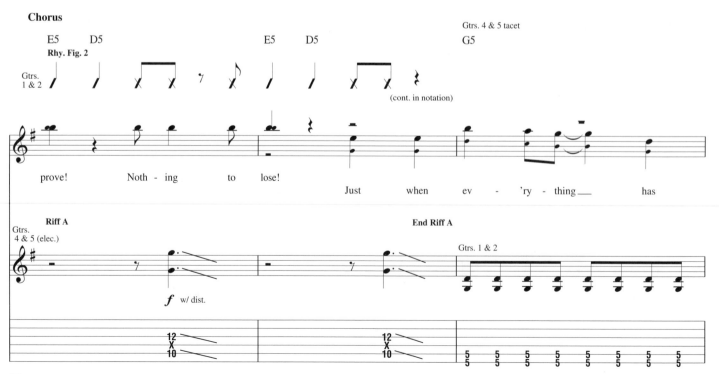

from the start____ that you'd take this trust and rip me a - part. ____

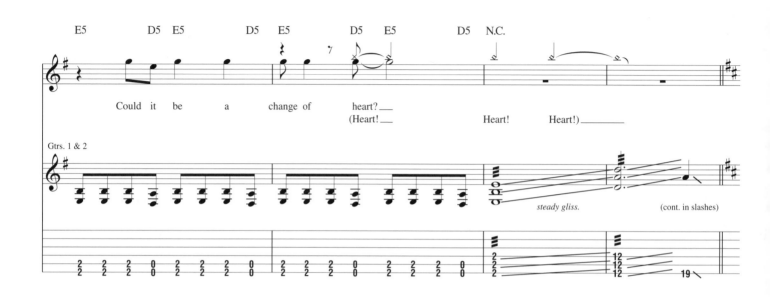

Could it be a change of heart?____
(Heart! ____ Heart! Heart!) ____

Gtrs. 1 & 2

steady gliss. (cont. in slashes)

Guitar Solo

Half time ♩ = 95

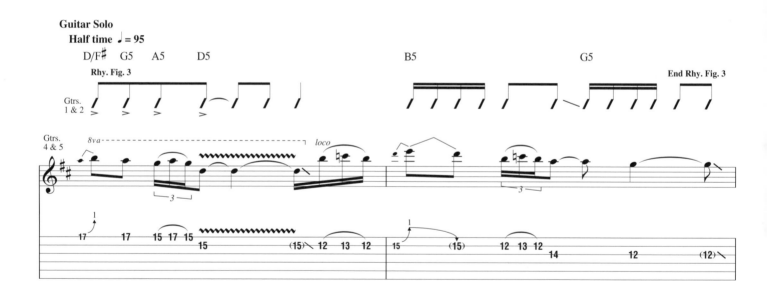

D/F♯ G5 A5 D5   B5   G5

Rhy. Fig. 3   End Rhy. Fig. 3

Gtrs. 1 & 2

Gtrs. 4 & 5

8va -   *loco*

Gtrs. 1 & 2: w/ Rhy. Fig. 3 (3 times)

D/F♯ G5 A5 D5   B5   G5

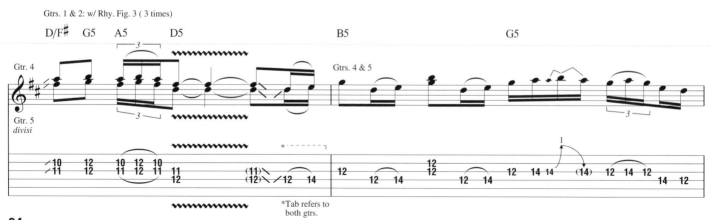

Gtr. 4

Gtrs. 4 & 5

Gtr. 5
divisi

*Tab refers to
both gtrs.

84

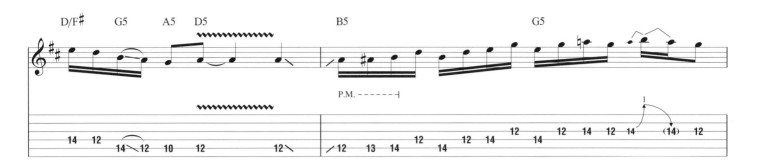

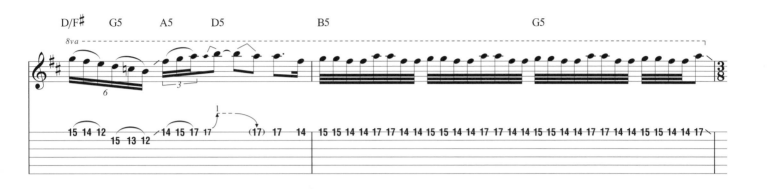

Interlude

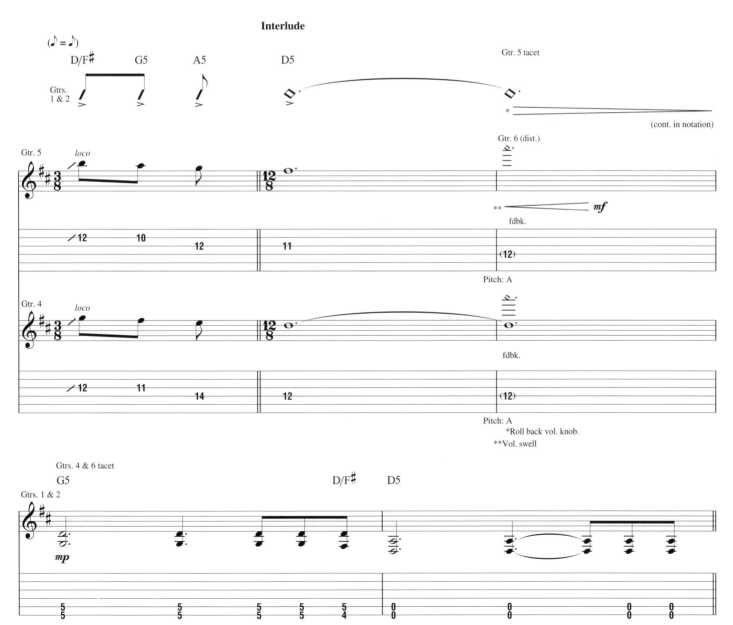

Outro

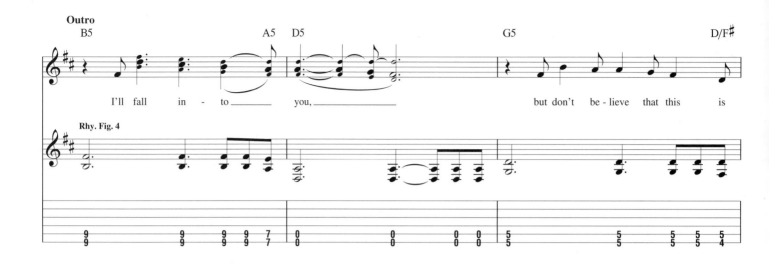

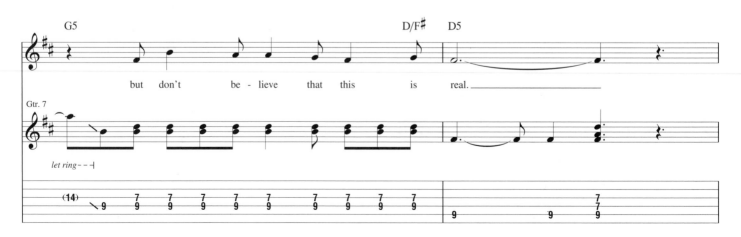

Guitar Notation Legend

Guitar Music can be notated three different ways: on a *musical staff*, in *tablature*, and in *rhythm slashes*.

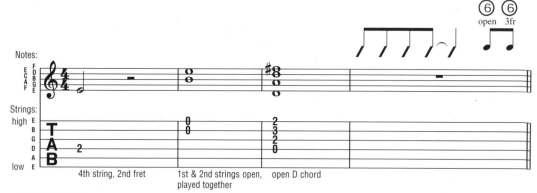

RHYTHM SLASHES are written above the staff. Strum chords in the rhythm indicated. Use the chord diagrams found at the top of the first page of the transcription for the appropriate chord voicings. Round noteheads indicate single notes.

THE MUSICAL STAFF shows pitches and rhythms and is divided by bar lines into measures. Pitches are named after the first seven letters of the alphabet.

TABLATURE graphically represents the guitar fingerboard. Each horizontal line represents a string, and each number represents a fret.

4th string, 2nd fret   1st & 2nd strings open, played together   open D chord

---

HALF-STEP BEND: Strike the note and bend up 1/2 step.

WHOLE-STEP BEND: Strike the note and bend up one step.

GRACE NOTE BEND: Strike the note and immediately bend up as indicated.

SLIGHT (MICROTONE) BEND: Strike the note and bend up 1/4 step.

BEND AND RELEASE: Strike the note and bend up as indicated, then release back to the original note. Only the first note is struck.

PRE-BEND: Bend the note as indicated, then strike it.

VIBRATO: The string is vibrated by rapidly bending and releasing the note with the fretting hand.

WIDE VIBRATO: The pitch is varied to a greater degree by vibrating with the fretting hand.

HAMMER-ON: Strike the first (lower) note with one finger, then sound the higher note (on the same string) with another finger by fretting it without picking.

PULL-OFF: Place both fingers on the notes to be sounded. Strike the first note and without picking, pull the finger off to sound the second (lower) note.

LEGATO SLIDE: Strike the first note and then slide the same fret-hand finger up or down to the second note. The second note is not struck.

SHIFT SLIDE: Same as legato slide, except the second note is struck.

TRILL: Very rapidly alternate between the notes indicated by continuously hammering on and pulling off.

TAPPING: Hammer ("tap") the fret indicated with the pick-hand index or middle finger and pull off to the note fretted by the fret hand.

NATURAL HARMONIC: Strike the note while the fret-hand lightly touches the string directly over the fret indicated.

PINCH HARMONIC: The note is fretted normally and a harmonic is produced by adding the edge of the thumb or the tip of the index finger of the pick hand to the normal pick attack.

PICK SCRAPE: The edge of the pick is rubbed down (or up) the string, producing a scratchy sound.

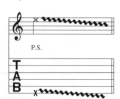

MUFFLED STRINGS: A percussive sound is produced by laying the fret hand across the string(s) without depressing, and striking them with the pick hand.

PALM MUTING: The note is partially muted by the pick hand lightly touching the string(s) just before the bridge.

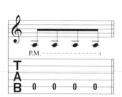

RAKE: Drag the pick across the strings indicated with a single motion.

TREMOLO PICKING: The note is picked as rapidly and continuously as possible.

VIBRATO BAR DIVE AND RETURN: The pitch of the note or chord is dropped a specified number of steps (in rhythm) then returned to the original pitch.

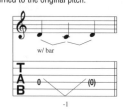

VIBRATO BAR SCOOP: Depress the bar just before striking the note, then quickly release the bar.

VIBRATO BAR DIP: Strike the note and then immediately drop a specified number of steps, then release back to the original pitch.